D1551505

M A R I N A T S V E T A E V A

▾   ▾   ▾

Moscow *in* *the* Plague Year

▾   ▾   ▾

Translated from the Russian by Christopher Whyte

a r c h i p e l a g o   b o o k s

English language translation © 2014 Christopher Whyte

First Archipelago Books Edition, 2014

Archipelago Books
232 3rd Street #A111
Brooklyn, NY 11215
www.archipelagobooks.org

Distributed by Random House
www.randomhouse.com

Library of Congress Cataloging-in-Publication Data
Tsvetaeva, Marina, 1892–1941, author.
[Poems. Selections. English. 2014]
Moscow in the plague year / Marina Tsvetaeva ; translated from the
Russian by Christopher Whyte. – First edition.
pages ; cm
ISBN 978-1-935744-96-2
I. Whyte, C. (Christopher), 1952– translator. II. Title.
PG3476.T75A2 2014
891.71'42 – dc23   2014000807

Cover art: "Jeanne Hebuterne with Hat and Necklace" by Amedeo Modigliani, 1917

Archipelago Books is grateful for the generous support from
Lannan Foundation, the National Endowment for the Arts, the New York State
Council on the Arts, a state agency, and the Mikhail Prokhorov Foundation
TRANSCRIPT Programme to Support Translations of Russian Literature.

Printed in the United States of America

Table of Contents

Sweet to be two of us – on just one horse   17

With airborne step   18

The morning dove has found a place   19

I'm giving you this comb so you'll remember   20

A mug, the tail end of the bread   22

Playacting

    1. An evening comes to mind. Early November   23

    2. So many wrists must   25

    3. Not love, but feverishness!   26

    4. With my shawl's ends I tie a knot   28

    5. To be my friend's forbidden, and I can't   29

    6. Do I kiss hair, or empty space?   30

    7. No peace for me until I hear   31

    8. As unforgettable as you're forgetful   32

    9. A brief chuckle   33

    10. For laughter, for worse   34

    11. Darling, I no longer need you   35

    12. Rose-coloured lips and beaver collar   37

    13. Flopped in an armchair, you can't be bothered   38

    14. Too much kissing has left your lips so   39

15. 'Give my daughter a kiss!'   40

16. Nothing at all, and yet immense   41

17. I blindly allowed transient lips and hands   42

18. More than kissing, we took aim   43

19. My friends! Family trinity! Closer   44

20. I hear two sibilants – here silk   46

21. Champagne is fuel for treachery   47

22. They're bored now that the drinking's done   48

23. Though it's unique, the sun parades through every city   49

24. Raise glasses to the Ace of Spades!   50

25. The very Devil took my side!   52

Into this drink I have dissolved   54

To Alya   55

Emperor and God! Concede forgiveness!   56

'The world will end with a deluge!'   58

Songs should be sung the way a man is loved   59

Things a tsar's son must do this   60

Accept my thanks, oh Lord   61

If there's sugar, you're pleased   62

A red bow for my hair!   63

Once you enchanted me   65

It's New Year. Roses in a heap   67

Kant was your food and drink, you raved about him   68

The Drummer Boy

    1. 'Drummer boy! Poor little lad!'   70

    2. Before my mother had me weaned   73

Withholding all the rest, the god of song   75

It's my pleasure to offer an example   76

A noise. I can't make out a word   77

I've loved you every day of my whole life   78

To P. Antokolsky   79

Not even one of you can understand   80

In Memoriam A. A. Stakhovich

    1. It wasn't bakeries being shut with seven   81

    2. Unostentatious signs   83

    3. By Novodevichy I search   84

    4. You and me in the Elysian Fields   86

Poems for Sonechka

    Envoi: To the Cigar Girl   87

    1. Before going off, a song!   88

    2. A little bird sang in the grove   90

    3. Raindrops patter on my window   92

    4. Raspberry-coloured rivulets begin   93

    5. As the railway carries me   96

    6. 'Tell us a story about spring!'   98

    7. Girl from the cigar factory   99

8. 'The burning sun's blackened your hands'   102

9. Don't lose your temper, angel from Heaven   103

10. Snow-white lily of the valley   104

[11] She sat on everybody's knees   106

To Alya   107

You think: 'Sheer downright fraudulence, like soldiers   108

Granny

1. When I get to be a granny   109

2. When finally the day arrived   112

You won't succeed in driving me away!   115

But on my forehead stars   116

To You Across One Hundred Years   118

I'd reached the point of shedding tears   121

Two trees long to reach each other   122

Consuela! Consolation! Don't   123

To Alya

1. In you there's not one drop of blood that's healthy   125

2. I never lift a finger when you fall   126

God! I'm alive! That means you aren't dead yet!   127

Somebody walks behind a plough   129

Masks and music. What's the third   130

My attic palace, my palatial attic!   131

I just can't get rid of you soon enough   133

There was a time when I was garlanded   135

You can decide: I've chopped up so much firewood   136

Want to know how my days proceed   137

We take the road of ordinary folk   138

To Balmont   140

My attic skylight up on high!   142

To Alya

    1. Sooner or later, creature of enchantment   143

    2. Vagabond, with no memories of a family!   144

    3. Little spirit of the home   145

Sitting in unlit carriages   147

The soul's immortal gift!   149

I want neither to eat, nor drink, nor live   150

I kissed him on the head without   151

Four-liners

    1. My rings upon so many hands   153

    2. Grandmothers love even the worst grand-daughters!   154

    3. Battling to get out of passion's rut   155

    4. A drop fell on my eyes   156

    5. All at once, while leafing through   157

    6. It'll happen tomorrow . . . The day after . . .   158

    7. The songbird always craves the grove   159

    8. You tell me I'm a whore – and but   160

9. Five-liner   161

10. I bring you my heart like a bird   162

11. But look, where tears are being shed   163

12. In your homes everything's kept under   164

13. I'm no rebel, I keep the rules. Whoever   165

14. Those entering the world clench small hands tight   166

15. No need for shame, my Russian land!   167

[16] While your eyes follow me into the grave   168

[17] All at once, while leafing through   169

[18] You brought me a fistful of rubies   170

[19] You tell me I'm a whore – you're right   171

[20] You tell me I'm a whore – but listen   172

[21] There was a robbery in your house   173

[22] Clatter of steps outside the window   174

[23] A step outside the door   175

[24] An entry in the guest book   176

Between Sunday and Saturday   177

A rose of flame in the blue sky   179

Pardon Love! Begging through the streets   180

A star above the cradle, and one more above the grave!   181

Born of debauch and separation   182

Getting your way thanks to a coach   183

My first grandmother bore four sons   184

I'll let the wind transport this book   185

You've travelled a long way, sleep sound in your new cell!   186

Psyche   187

His gown is coloured raspberry   189

She creeps up imperceptibly   191

Old-Fashioned Deference   192

Equally young, equally ragged   194

Do I love you?   195

From seven until seven   197

'I've sunk so low, and you're so wretched'   199

You'd take him for an emperor's son   200

Dying, I'll regret the gypsy songs   201

Ballad of the Outcast Girl   202

After H. Heine   204

But when I come again into this world   206

Two hands, each lowered gently   207

A Son   208

To Vyacheslav Ivanov

    1. Your finger's writing in the sand   210

    2. Your finger's writing in the sand   211

    3. A favourite, not a paramour   212

To N(ikolay) N(ikolayevich) V(ysheslavtsev)

    1. Along great, silent roads   214

    2. All of the sea needs all of the sky   215

    3. Odour of England – of the sea   216

4. *All we have's one hour of time*   218

5. *A friend eyes have not seen, ears have not heard*   220

6. *My way doesn't lead past your house*   222

7. *Sympathy in my neighbour's eyes*   224

8. *I'd sooner give my life than sacrifice*   225

9. *Bagged and under water – that's real courage!*   226

10. *So trivial, so frivolous*   227

11. *Repulsed by a blow to the chest*   228

12. *Having bid all passions farewell*   229

13. *You've no end of complaints at my behaviour!*   231

14. *Don't hurry to reach a judgement!*   232

[14a] *And yet for half an hour we two*   233

15. *When it's unbearable – the pain a woman*   234

16. *Filled with wonder, totally enraptured*   237

17. *Nailed to the pillar of shame of my old*   238

18. *Even though nailed to the pillar of shame*   239

19. *This is what you wanted. – Yes. – So be it*   241

20. *With this my hand, whose praises seafarers*   242

21. *If stanzas cannot help, nor constellations*   243

22. *You cannot do your dirty work quite so*   245

23. *Some are made of stone, and some of clay*   246

24. *Just take it all, I don't need any of it*   247

25. Death of the Dancing Girl   248

26. I've not been dancing, so I'm not to blame 249

27. With the eyes of a witch under a spell 250

My humble roof! Smoke from a beggar's fire! 251

Here I sit, bereft of light, and bread 252

I wrote it on a blackboard of dark slate 253

Shadows have overtaken half a house 254

My pity goes to everyone! 255

I place my hand upon my heart and swear 256

Half of the window has been opened 258

Afterword 259

Translator's Note 267

Moscow *in the* Plague Year

Sweet to be two of us – on just one horse,
in the one dinghy, riding one wave,
sweet when the two of us chew the same crust –
sweetest of all when we share the same pillow.

November 1st 1918

▾   ▾   ▾

With airborne step –
the sign of a clear conscience –
with airborne step
and resonant song

God set me down alone amidst
the world's immensity: 'You're not
a woman', he said, 'but a bird.
Your task, therefore – to fly and sing!'

November 1st 1918

The morning dove has found a place
to perch on my right shoulder, while
the eagle owl of night has found
a place to perch upon my left.

Like Kazan's emperor, I pass
knowing I have no cause to fear –
enemies having joined in league
to offer me common defence!

November 2nd 1918

I'm giving you this comb so you'll remember
me longer than an hour, lad, or a year.

Little gold combs got invented for that –
so young lovers don't forget their girls.

To stop the one I love drinking without me –
comb, little comb for straightening my hair!

This one is special, there's no other like it –
pulled through my hair, its teeth feel just like strings!

As soon as you touch it, a shiver will run
all down my body, but nobody else's.

To stop the one I love sleeping without me –
comb, little comb for straightening my hair!

So that every inch he puts between us
can seem to him a mile of burning sweat,

each mile as he returns seems like an inch –
little gold combs got invented for that.

To stop the one I love living without me –
comb, darling comb, with all your seven teeth!

November 2nd 1918

▾   ▾   ▾

A mug, the tail end of the bread,
a raspberry out of the punnet,
moonlight through the attic window –
that's how far our banquet reaches!

As a bonus, offer me
a lad I can get warmed up with –
even when no bread's included,
I can never hope to pay!

November 2nd 1918

PLAYACTING

Dedication:
To an actor, trying to pass for an angel, or an angel,
trying to pass for an actor – it makes no difference,
since in 1919 tenderness towards Your Worship, and
not snow, had me in thrall

I

An evening comes to mind. Early November.
Rain falling, foggy. Underneath the streetlamp,
your gentle features, alien, uncertain,
pallid and blurred as in a Dickens novel.
A shivering as of winter seas within me. . . .
Your gentle features underneath the streetlamp.

The wind howled, and the stair we climbed unravelled . . .
My eyes were riveted upon your lips;
I stood, twisting my fingers, almost laughing,
the version of a Muse in miniature,
as blameless as the evening hour was late . . .
The wind howled, and the stair we climbed unravelled.

You overwhelmed me from beneath tired eyelids
with hopes that had no chance of being fulfilled.
Touching upon your lips, my gaze slid onwards . . .
Thus does an angel, wearied by the robes
that camouflage its hidden sanctity,
enchant the world from underneath tired eyelids.

Another night from one of Dickens' novels.
Rain falls again. Again there's no escape
for me, for you. A downpour in the gutters.
The staircase flashes by . . . Again, those lips . . .
Those same steps hurry off into the night,
going who knows where, in one of Dickens' novels.

November 2nd 1918

2

So many wrists must
have dallied and curled.
What was it made my
wrist special for you?

Turning in circles –
cat with a mouse!
Falcon, it's eyes we
use, not lips, to look!

November 19th 1918

3

Not love, but feverishness!
Playful combat, sly, mendacious.
Sickening one day, sweet the next,
at death's door, then alive again.

Battle rages. Both enjoy it.
He is smart – but she's no fool!
To me the hero and first lady
are equally captivating.

A shepherd's staff – or else a sword?
Sidelines, combat – or a dance?
One step forwards, three steps back,
one step backwards, three ahead.

Honeyed lips, trust-inspiring eyes
then, all at once, the eyebrow darts.
Pretending in the place of love,
absolute hypocrisy!

The fruit of these (uncommitted –
between brackets!) sins will be
fluttering pages, in a stack,
of impassioned poetry.

November 20th 1918

4

With my shawl's ends I tie a knot
around your melancholy.
Watch me as, shawlless, I proceed
singing from square to square.

The curse has been dispelled. From now
on you're in thrall to me!

November 20th 1918

5

To be my friend's forbidden, and I can't
be loved! Exquisite eyes keep all at bay!

Longboats are meant to sail, and mills to grind.
Is stopping hearts in orbit your vocation?

My notebook will make sure you never win.
Should one lavish such feeling on mere acting?

Love's cross is heavy. We won't try to lift it.
Yesterday's gone, and we shall dig its grave.

November 20th 1918

6

Do I kiss hair, or empty space?
Eyelids, or the wind's breath on them?
Lips, or your breath upon my lips?
No way to tell, or break the charm.

One thing's sure: a whole history
of bliss is contained in this cloudlet
of breath dispersing, epic thronged
with emperors, haunting, many-stringed.

All that is earthly's doomed to pass,
including you and love, my friend!
Your voice and locks will survive in
my song's attacks, each shadowed string.

November 22nd 1918

7

No peace for me until I see,
no peace until I hear,
no peace until I catch your gaze,
until I hear your words.

A tiny slip set the sum wrong.
Who'll sort out the mistake?
That ever so sweet smile of yours
dissolved my bitterness.

My grandchildren will write a label
for my ashes: 'off her rocker'.
Weakening yet stubborn, I repeat:
No peace until I see, I hear . . .

November 23rd 1918

8

As unforgettable as you're forgetful,
you resemble your smile! Shall I
repeat it? Golden morning lacks
your loveliness! In all the universe
your like cannot be found – love's youthful
captive, goblet modelled by Cellini.

Shall I make an old-fashioned declaration?
The tenderness with which I love you, Sir,
is unmatched. – In the chimney the wind howls.
I stare into the glowing fire, my chin
cupped in my hands. My love for you
is just as guiltless as a child's.

But nothing lasts! Life will unclasp the palms
pressing against my temples. Youthful captive,
love will release you. My voice, though, has wings,
and will proclaim, inspired, so all can hear,
how once you dwelt amongst us on the earth,
as unforgettable as you're forgetful!

November 25th 1918

9

A brief chuckle
reveals your teeth.
You screw your eyes up, playful, impudent.
I love you! Love your teeth, your lips!
(I've told you so a thousand times!)

Falling in love has worked again.
Not to forget your lovely hands!
Don't worry, I pay off my debts
with the soul's coins, that can't be changed.

Just laugh! Tonight I want to dream
your cheeks dimpling before you smile.
Nothing comes gratis. Fair exchange!
A penny, a sovereign: a verse, a laugh.

November 27th 1918

10

For laughter, for worse,
rather than falling
for sound common sense,
for clarity, sun-drenched,

for whiteness of snow,
I gave this heart
whose homeland is Sparta
to midnight mirages,

a flute-player's flattery,
thoughts of no consequence.
Do you remember the
Spartan boy's fox cub?

Simpler concealing it
under a tunic than
hiding the tenderness
I'm overwhelmed by!

December 1st 1918

II

Darling, I no longer need you.
Not because no letter in
your hand came with the morning post.

Not because, construing lines
prompted from me by such aching,
you'll inevitably chuckle.

(From me, to you. For our eyes only!
In theory. At least to start with.
You'll get help decoding them.)

And not because your curls touch
against my cheek. I'm a past master
at reading out both roles!

Not because my punctuation's
so faulty you will breathe a sigh
of deprecation, bent over

the page. My handwriting's so hard
to read. And then, it's poetry!
Your eyes fall shut, as if in concert.

No darling, this is much more straight-
forward than getting cross with you.

The reason I no longer need
you – the real reason – is I just
don't need you any longer!

December 3rd 1918

12

Rose-coloured lips and beaver collar
acted out an amorous night.
Love completed the triangle.

Impudent, light-hearted smiles,
collar strutting in beaver fur,
and Love, waiting, without a word.

13

Flopped in an armchair, you can't be bothered
lifting a finger. I'm kneeling beside you,
attentive to your next commands.

Half-asleep, your arm is dangling.
Noiselessly I lift your hand,
the Chinese ring upon one finger.

The ring has been cleaned using chalk.
Happy about it? Don't thank me!
Love's the one you need to thank.

December 5th 1918

14

Too much kissing has left your lips so
yielding, and me like a beggar.
Am I alone? More like the thousandth!
More conquest than a conqueror.

Is this love, or feasting one's eyes?
The pen's whim? Or a primal cause?
A languor such as angels feel?
Or cheating natural to actors?

Grief to the soul, enchantment for the eyes,
swift-moving pen . . . Does it make any difference
what names we call these lips by, if they keep
on yielding, and the kissing never stops?

December 1918

15

'Give my daughter a kiss!'
That's all I asked. You're stingy.
No point getting upset.
I draw the line right here.

Were you the one who had
a boy, an only son,
I would have said the same
to you: 'Give him a kiss!'

Nothing at all, and yet immense –
so simple, yet a mystery.
The woman who forgot her vows
came back to them before night fell.

Demure as a nun clothed in white,
eyes never lifted from the ground,
the one no-one could put a stop to
stopped herself before night fell.

beginning of January 1919

17

I blindly allowed transient lips and hands
to destroy the eternity I hoped for.
I sing of them, those transient lips and hands,
as I take leave of my eternal soul.

Eternal life's dumb rumbling's growing fainter.
But now and then, when day's about to break,
a secret voice resounds out of dark skies:
'Woman! Remember your eternal soul!'

end of December 1918

18

More than kissing, we took aim.
We did not shape our breath to words.
Maybe you never lived, maybe
only your coat hung on the chair.

Your youthful form may well have lain
for years beneath a level slab.
I felt that I was made of wax,
dead girl upon a bed of roses.

Hand on my heart, I note no beat.
It's easy without passion, torment!
What, in the world, they call a lovers'
rendezvous came down to this.

beginning of January 1919

19

My friends! Family trinity! Closer
than blood could ever be!
My friends in a Moscow turned Soviet,
Jacobin, home to Marat!

I start with you, impassioned Antokolsky,
the frigid Muses' pet –
never forget the name I bear was once
a Polish gentlewoman's.

Not to mention – guilty, chill, fraternal –
Zavadsky, whom a mesh
of obstacles put beyond reach, unrivalled
in intelligence!

Rounding things off, hero amidst dissemblers,
immune to everyday
concerns, forgetting all names, even
his own! – Alekseyev!

Practising the ancient art of self-
effacement, the proverbial black diamond,
I lend you an indulgent, mournful ear
as Sibyls did of old – and like Georges Sand.

January 13th 1919

20

I hear two sibilants – here silk,
the snowstorm outside. Beating soul
and breathing blood. We both got what
we wanted – you, my rapture and a bed
of snow, and me, death-dealing love for you.

January 27th 1919

21

Champagne is fuel for treachery.
But fill the glass and drink it down!
You'll fall asleep in the dark tomb
with no roses for chains!

You're not my husband and won't be,
your head is growing blurred . . .
But our novel's hero mustn't
waver in his love!

22

They're bored now that the drinking's done.
You've no idea how I rejoice!
You're the master, I'm the mistress.
The main thing is – we are the same!

Don't kid yourself! The grim chill when
you swallow tells you that my lips
pressed upon yours. Or was it just
the froth of abundant champagne?

Some drinking sprees are fit for gods.
This one of mine is justified:
it brought the champagne lie of love
without the treacle of love's truth!

23

Though it's unique, the sun parades through every city.
The sun belongs to me. I'm not going to relinquish

an hour, a beam, a glance to anyone.
Let the cities perish in endless night!

It's in my hands! Just let it dare keep turning!
No matter if I burn hands, lips, and heart!

Lost in eternal night . . . I rush off on its tracks.
I won't relinquish you, my sun, to anyone!

February 1919

24

Raise glasses to the Ace of Spades!
Raise them to this sodality
of boasting and of broken trust!
Encounters on dark bridges, under
every single streetlamp – love!

I sing the praises of the lying
blood flowing through my faithless veins,
the faithless lovers peopling
the future I've ahead of me!

Drink to the playactor, to the
red band in my uproarious locks!
Drink to the children sitting at
their school desks. May they grow to be
more fatuous still than we once were!

With youth's last gasp, beneath the shade
of dry fig trees, I sing the women
fated to be your lovers in
the future you've ahead of you!

Moscow, March 1919

25

The very Devil took my side!
While I was tempted by the lure
of red lips at the midnight hour,
there the blood that flowed was red.

On the Don's sands a superhuman
legion was being decimated
while I fraternised with a band
of actors in plague-stricken Moscow.

Faithlessness has a pliant backbone.
Such multitudes answered the call
[…] of my kisses
[…] of my verses.

The Devil stepped in to make sure
my conscience wouldn't burn beneath
my shawl. Giddy, plague-stricken night
prevailed, no hint of dawns or days.

Only in earliest twilight did
an angel bend over a woman,
riverside reed, and let tears fall
because she'd forgotten a face.

March 1919

▼　　▼　　▼

Into this drink I have dissolved
a fistful of burnt hair for you
to stop you eating, stop you singing,
stop you drinking, stop you sleeping,

to make sure that your youth is joyless,
so your sugar won't be sweet,
so that after dark no young
woman cuddles in your arms.

Just as these gold curls of mine
were transformed to ashen grey,
so your years as a young man
will be cold and white as winter.

So that you'll go blind and deaf,
dry out like a clump
of moss, depart, a sigh.

November 3rd 1918

TO ALYA

Although you still have both father and mother,
you nonetheless remain one of Christ's orphans.

Though you were born in a whirlpool of wars
you too will make your way unto the Jordan.

A key is quite superfluous when Christ's
doors open so that Christ's orphan can enter.

November 5th 1918

▼   ▼   ▼

Emperor and God! Concede forgiveness!
Puny, misled, sinful, maddened,
sucked into a fearsome vortex,
seduced, a victim of deception . . .

Emperor and God! Inflict no brutal
punishment on Stenka Razin!

Emperor! The Lord will reward you!
Too long we've been howling like orphans!
More than enough of us have died!
Emperor's son! Forgive the brigand!

Our father's house has many doors.
Have mercy upon Stenka Razin!

Razin! Razin! Your tale's ended.
The red beast's been conquered and bound.
His fearsome teeth are broken, but
on account of his dark life,

of his senseless daring, too –
undo Stenka Razin's bonds!

Motherland! River source and mouth!
Joy! Old Russia's fragrance renewed!
Eyes that grew dim can shine once more!
Russian hearts can celebrate!

Emperor and God! Today's a
holiday! Set Stenka Razin free!

Moscow, first anniversary of the October Revolution

▼   ▼   ▼

'The world will end with a deluge!'
'The world will end with a fire!'
At midnight, daughter and mother
disputing like water and fire.

'The Holy Ghost – a pigeon by a lake,
a little white dove perching on a branch.'
'No, more a tongue of flame above
a [light-brown] head – and a fire in the throat.'

November 7th 1918

▾   ▾   ▾

Songs should be sung the way a man is loved –
joyously! With all one's energy!
What does it matter if they are forgotten?
God's the one I'm singing for – not people!

Songs should be sung the way the heart keeps beating –
singing is life . . .

November 9th 1918

▼   ▼   ▼

Things a tsar's son must do:
be mighty and be good
[...]
honour hungry ribs.

Stand by his last soldier,
drink with the last beggar,
sleep [...]
in boots, his sword unsheathed.

More things he has to do:
get up when midnight strikes,
proceed on a white path
right to the mountain top . . .

Bend over an abyss,
toss something into it . . .
Never retrace his steps –
things a tsar's son must do!

November 9th 1918

Accept my thanks, oh Lord
for ocean, for dry land,
enchantments of the flesh,
the spirit that won't die,

for this fire in the blood,
water that brings refreshment.
Accept my thanks for love,
and for the weather, too.

November 9th 1918

▼   ▼   ▼

If there's sugar, you're pleased,
if there's none, you complain,
for a moment it's here,
the next moment it's gone –
sweet, but sickening too!

You, suffering, are a salty sea!
Nourishment too,
slaking of thirst,
turning my head,
serving your turn!

November 9th 1918

A red bow for my hair!
A red bow for my hair!
The man I love's on guard,
doing sentry duty.

When the wind blows cold,
when the moon is chill,
he stands outside the tent,
salt pillar in the field.

I sneak up quietly,
he cries aloud: 'Password?'
'It's me!' 'Move on, the king
is sleeping soundly now!'

'It's me, my heart! This is
your own heart calling you!'
'No time for joking here,
my rifle's in my hand.'

'But would you let your king
sleep through the hour for mass?'
'For the third and last time –
move on, I tell you, move!'

A shot rings out, noiseless
I slump upon the heath.
The sentry looks northwards
and then looks to the south,

to the east, to the west.
No yawning while on duty!
A red bow for my hair!
A red bow for my hair!

November 10th 1918

▼   ▼   ▼

Once you enchanted me,
now I've no time for you.
I've found a prodigal
son to replace you.

No courts, no palaces
but forests, wastelands,
no soldiers or armies –
sands of the sea.

That's where we're walking now,
next with the forest wolves.
Every night a new bed –
gravel and then bare stone.

That's what my new man likes,
as clear as Eastertide:
one night the moon's our lamp,
next the stars light our way.

No man could ride like him,
prince welcome everywhere –
one look into my eyes –
armies got left behind!

November 10th 1918

It's New Year. Roses in a heap.
Ageing peer in an opulent frame.
Did you bring me a ribbon? Daisy's
a woman of importance now.

She alights from far-reaching wings.
The red ribbon's no longer needed.
Here no-one has a problem with
respecting seraphim and students.

What? You can't depart alone!
Take me off to Malta with you.
Such impertinence, combined
with a matchless contralto voice!

It's New Year! The New Year's come in!
Chit for a Smithson in her bouquet.
A trembling seraph from Rossetti
stands hungering at my front door!

November 10th 1918

▼   ▼   ▼

Kant was your food and drink, you raved about him.
I went around wearing a bright red ribbon.
Diamonds and [dandies] were in short supply.
[...]

All that we had to eat were peas and lentils.
One day you brought a singer to the house
up off the street – drenched and melodious,
like a small bird. We shared our dinner with her.

And then – [...] as gods do –
all we could talk about was scalding grog
while, shivering, we stretched our legs into
the black hole where a fire had once been lit.

Our tipple water – [...] a drinking bout!
You said: 'Sister, it's time for you to sing!'
She sang a song whose subject was a shapely
horsewoman and a king young in years.

You said that love and friendship could be sisters.
She tied her still damp, coloured ribbon in
my hair and it flared up – enchanting island!
[…]

We kissed each other. Next we played at dice.
The two of us fell asleep on the coal bunker,
relinquishing our one and only mattress
to the guest with the melodious voice.

November 10th 1918

THE DRUMMER BOY

I

Drummer boy! Poor little lad!
Look neither to the right nor left!
March on at the army's head
with God's thunder on your chest.

No mercenary – all you bear
is on your chest, not on your back!
First to be hurled into death's jaws,
moving on foot – like on a horse!

Your mother sped through the ripe rye,
your mother appealed to the clouds,
and implored: 'Mother of God,
let nothing happen to my son!'

Your wretched mother's handkerchief
hasn't stopped waving from the window.
'Where are you, sunshine of the camp?
its scarlet flower, where are you?'

As compensation, a huge freedom,
his oldest brother's an apprentice,
middle a peasant, third in school
while he's already in the army!

Battle's finished – you're not injured,
cause for joy and feeling proud
when the camp-follower you fancy
brings over your glass of beer!

NCO grumbles: 'Look, young lad,
starting soon's a bad idea!
Early start and early finish!'
Who'll knock the beer back when I'm dead?

But if death the she-wolf takes me
I won't run away – that's all!
The Emperor will get his cities,
his drummer boy lie in the snow.

Or at the bottom of the sea.
The devil take me, I don't care!
As long as he's the one who puts
the cross on my chest with his hands!

November 11th 1918

2

Before my mother had me weaned
I beat on my drum day and night.
She said the din would drive her deaf.
My father slapped me on the back.

My mother weeps and sighs and grieves.
For me, my father's word is law:
'Let him go serve the Emperor,
he's born to be a drummer boy.'

We conquered countries in their hundreds,
pocketed capitals in passing.
At Austerlitz two elements
were crucial – sunlight, and my drum.

So many of us breathed our last
to bring the Emperor victory!
My drumskin found cause to rejoice!
I'm born to be a drummer boy!

We got the German in a corner.
A horseman. Salute from my drum.
Three-cornered hat. His arms are folded.
– Your age? – Ten. – Sure it's that much, rogue?

He was alone. A smallish figure.
Now's he's raised higher than the sun!
– Mum's the word, lad! Mum's the word!
You're born to be a drummer boy!

God's Mother took her grace from us,
kept distant from the Moscow wolves.
Worse and still worse. Our Emperor captured,
his faithful army in despair.

My favourite chum has fallen silent.
These fingers nailed him to the wall.
Nobody's hand can beat him now.
I did it to the manner born!

November 12th 1918

Withholding all the rest, the god of song
made me the gift of a nightingale's throat.
A nightingale's throat! [...]
Warble on, nightingale passion of mine!

I strain all my throat's strings until they snap!
If I entered the world a nightingale,
it wasn't so I could preserve my throat!
[...]

November 20th 1918

▼   ▼   ▼

It's my pleasure to offer an example
by living simply, like a pendulum,
the sun, the calendar, an anchoress,
slender, saintly, wise like all God's creatures.

To know my soul's my guide, fights at my side,
to enter unannounced, a ray, a glance,
to live the very way I write, succinctly,
as God commanded, and my friends do not.

November 22nd 1918

A noise. I can't make out a word.
Something draws close. Darkness again.
I know that sound comes from the fields,
or somewhere higher. From my heart?

'Onwards to torment by fire!'
Clothed in rippling sheep's fleece,
I raise my hands towards the sky
like, long ago, a certain girl . . .

1918–1939

▾   ▾   ▾

I've loved you every day of my whole life,
like a huge shadow cast on me, or like
the ancient smoke of Arctic villages.

I've loved you every hour of my whole life.
Your lips, your eyes, though, are superfluous.
It all began – and ended – without you.

I can recover something – a rainbow
of sounds, a giant collar, untouched snow,
horns lowered against a backdrop of stars . . .

They cast a shadow over half the skyline . . .
The ancient smoke of Arctic villages . . .
I get it now: you are a northern stag.

December 7th 1918

TO P. ANTOKOLSKY

This ring of iron I bestow on you
confers insomnia, rapture and despair.
You will no longer look girls in the face,
forgetting what the word 'tenderness' means.

The head you lift, amidst its maddening
curls, will be a goblet brimming over
while, on your hand, this iron ornament
will turn you back to coal, ashes and dust.

When Love itself, become a burning coal,
nestles against your head's prophetic curls,
say not a word, just press this iron ring
upon its sunburnt finger to your lips –

a talisman against which reddening mouths
are powerless, first link in your chain mail,
so that, an oak tree in the storm of days,
you'll stand alone – God in his iron ring!

March 1919

Not even one of you can understand –
you'd never want to, couldn't go so far! –
how, when sleeping is impossible,
passionate conscience gnaws at my young life!

How, choking on the pillow, it emits
alarm signals, keeps whispering the same words . . .
What sort of a thrice-cursèd Hell my foolish
ha'penny worth of sin has turned into!

March 1919

IN MEMORIAM A. A. STAKHOVICH

A Dieu – mon âme,
Mon corps – au Roy,
Mon coeur – aux Dames,
L'honneur – pour moi.

I

It wasn't bakeries being shut with seven
locks, or ice coating the stoves, that sent
you, nobleman of Russia, to your grave
with perfect posture and a lordly step!

Fate took its course. The old world was ablaze.
It fell to courtiers to cut wood. The mob
had its heyday . . . In your vicinity
one still could breathe the eighteenth century.

The mob tore off the roofs from palaces
to get its hands on what it longed for, while
amidst general devastation, you
taught young men *maintien, tenue* and *bon ton.*

Rather than offer the mob bread and salt,
like a disgruntled courtier you made
a cross with your incomparable hands,
in the black realm where toil leaves callouses.

March 1919

2

Unostentatious signs
of my lofty distress,
two waxen tears remain
on my mittens' dark blue.

Thick clouds of breath inside
the freezing chapel where
we shook, air from our lips
mingling with blue incense.

Did you notice, friend, least
ostentatious of all,
my breath's smoke mingling with
the smoke of other breaths?

Your peerless hands were famed
throughout your native land.
Don't take it amiss, me
standing in mittens here!

March 1919

3

By Novodevichy I search
the wilderness for a grave's dip.
Snowdrifts, potholes, snowdrifts. This
is Moscow in nineteen nineteen.

Below, incomparable hands
form a cross they chose to form
upon a heart which, living nobly,
earned the right to cease to live.

A lamentable entourage!
Moscow detailed flooded roads,
cold and hunger to act as guard
of honour at your funeral.

'Who died, then?' – 'Comrade, on your way!
Nothing that you could understand.
An ancient family – noble blood –
a courtier – better than the rest.'

By Novodevichy I trudge

[…]

My prayer – a meeting in the blessed
warmth of the Elysian Fields!

March 1919

4

You and me in the Elysian Fields
while, far beneath, the world's consigned to flames.
[…] seas resembling puddles, and
Russia, our fated native land, where in
the cemetery by Novodevichy
our pitiful remains are laid to rest.

That's where we last met! But in what a context!
Some countries don't need bayonets or sacks!
Two centuries behind the times, in that
world children shouted for equality
while we two, arrogant as courtiers, loomed,
no less ghosts then than we've become today.

What does it mean to us? Russia? Black domes.
Consigning our bodies as hostages
to that insatiable worm, the black mob,
Poet and Courtier tenderly conversed,
laughing-stocks in a state of snows, but gods
where gods join kings to form a heavenly choir!

March 1919

Envoi: To the Cigar Girl

The driver of the coach I've hired
won't wait. The wind itself is in
a hurry. Here's one further little
gift to remember me by.

1919

I

Before going off, a song!
One from the heart!
My rosy lips today,
tomorrow yours!

Everybody loves
a pretty rose!
Lots of us around –
like me, like you.

Someone steals a rose
that was his friend's.
Problem is, the rose
risks getting torn!

Rather than fight
over rosy lips –
better to take turns
kissing the lads!

Hundreds of us in
pursuit of one.
Make the best of him
while he's still yours.

April 21st 1919

2

A little bird sang in the grove,
an organ-grinder at the window:
Don't believe him, he'll betray you,
don't believe a single word!

Drunken devils from the winecask
kept the chorus going strong:
Hi there, girlie! All they paid him
to betray you was a farthing!

From the meadow the cows mooed:
She didn't half enjoy herself!
The mongrels at the gateway raised
a cheer for her, the bloody fool!

She wondered if it might be best
to drown herself. A bearded crone
said: 'Girlie, not a word of that!
Water will wash your pain away!

There now, dry your shining eyes.
Get a comb and sort your hair.
The man you were in love with dumped you?
Find yourself another one!'

3

Raindrops patter on my window,
a worker scrapes at his machine.
I made my living singing through
the streets – you were a prince's son.

I sang about how badly life
had treated me. No pennies came
down from the gilded balcony –
no, I was honoured with a smile.

Word reached your father, and he tore
the medal from your uniform,
then sent a lackey out to chase
the little slut from his courtyard.

That evening I got roaring drunk,
imagining a blessed world
in which my father was the prince,
and you were singing through the streets!

April 24th 1919

4

Raspberry-coloured rivulets begin
trickling across the snow at break of day.
Not hiding the emotion in my voice,
I'll sing the story of a darling girl,

educated in a glittering hothouse
(she could have been some special kind of plant),
a school for girls out of the upper classes
whose breeding had to be impeccable.

If anyone pronounced the word 'fiancé,'
she plunged her white face in her pinafore.
On school's last day, she read a poem out
with the heir to the throne among her listeners.

She led a prankster cavalcade of orphans
down to the church, along the boulevard.
And then a hussar came back home on leave,
an eldest son, pride of his family.

Hussar! She'd hardly finished saying goodbye
to dolls! Still in our cradles, we start hoping
for a hussar! Our wildest dream! So back
to basics! Fingers crossed she'll pass the test!

Let's watch her as, virginal, rosy-cheeked,
she picks a blossom, puts it in a vase.
Can she count on the trusty old trump cards?
Patience, a sung romance, the *contredanse*?

The creature was bloodless from head to foot,
white as her handkerchief from top to toe.
That's what she waved goodbye with when he left.
His helmet's plume answered her from the saddle.

Then all at once she crumpled at the feet
of an old crone, who couldn't be more proper.
Stamping impatiently, the count himself
lowered her from the steps onto the snow.

Her father had deserved a better daughter!
Carrying only a pathetic bundle
she left the Royal Foundlings' Hospital.
What options did she have? So she entrusted

her rosy little cheeks to butterflies
without one serious thought inside their heads,
then put her wretched innocence at the
disposal of His Majesty's armed forces.

Next she rented her beauty out on credit
to artists with no notion about morals
and led the mutineering mob over
the bridge together with a thief – a jailbird . . .

Some fisherman, on a beach far away,
stumbled on the remnants of two shoes . . .
We're all familiar with the story, it's
been told before. My song deserves two tears.

April 1919

5

As the railway carries me
far from evil thoughts of love,
as the engine pants and puffs

and its morose hooter sounds,
I can't get from my head the thought
I was a fool to say goodbye

to your smiles, that were so sweet,
to your hands, your gloves, your face
I'm never going to see again

or to your softly-murmured words,
to the feet I heard hurrying
past my home and down the street.

So goodbye, villain, seducer
and goodbye to you, my hills
looking down on […] Moscow –

Moscow can go to the Devil,
and me, too, along with it,
let the whole world go to Hell!

Pour out, tears, pour out, pour out,
keep twisting and turning, rails,
moan, hooter, keep moaning on . . .

Maybe once I get abroad
I'll forget how cruel fate was
in somebody else's arms.

6

'Tell us a story about spring!'
That's what her grandchildren want.
The old woman shakes her head,
all she says in answer is:
'Spring is sinful,
spring is awful.'

'Tell us a story about love!'
sings her grandson, the one who's
handsomer than all the rest.
Staring at the fire, she answers:
'Love is sinful,
love is awful!'

In the yard, as twilight falls,
innocence's song rings out:
'Love is sinful,
love is awful . . .'

7

Girl from the cigar factory
who sets all Seville laughing, dancing!
What's your fancy in that lanky
bloke not from around these parts?

'Don't find fault with his long legs
He gets where he wants the fastest.'
Herons' legs are just as long –
to keep them upright in the marsh!

So what if his hands are white?
Cats have white paws, just the same.
'Don't find fault with his white hands!
Must be great when they caress you!'

So what if his hair is fair? Don't
frothing wave tips have bright curls?
Wreaths of smoke have them as well,
and our chickens have white feathers!

He doesn't sing when he gets up
and when he goes to bed, he hasn't
touched a drink. Keep clear of him!
He hides away from women and

the light of day in churches and
in cellars, shunning sunlight like
a knife blade, shunning smiles as if
they were the plague. Keep clear of him!

Bashfulness and modesty
look good on a girl like you,
they're the get-up that suits her best –
things that would disgrace a man.

A man who borrows nothing from
his friends won't give his girlfriends much.
He's never called upon the Jews –
he'll end up like a Jew himself.

Girl from the cigar factory,
darling sweetheart, cute and youthful,
find another destination
for those lovely lips of yours.

They're as beautiful as roses
but they're sure to fade tomorrow.
They'll look mournful on a ghost's face,
stone is hard for living souls.

Moscow-Vanves, 1919–1937

8

'The burning sun's blackened your hands.
Your legs, though, are brighter than glass . . .
Roll me a cigar, cigar girl
so I can puff out my love.'

Passers-by say: 'Take a look at
those eyes of his! So handsome, bright!'
And my murmured answer: 'Smoke did
that. I smoked my girl away!'

Spring 1919

9

Don't lose your temper, angel from Heaven,
if it turns out that the truth was a lie.
People don't look to the wind for straight answers,
nightingales singing can distort the truth.

1919

10

Snow-white lily of the valley,
little crimson rose!
Tender words from all of them:
'You're the one for me!

Your face is like an icon's face,
voice like a singing bird's . . .'
Gently, gently rocking her,
seated on his knees.

The pendulum on God's clock swings
first right and then left.
The same refrain kept coming back:
'You're the one for me!'

God's counsels are unshakable,
the way has been marked out.
Baby girls never grow up,
what's free can't be restrained.

One the girls don't get to kiss
wagged his little finger:
when the lad had left, God's angel
stood up from the bed.

'You'll blossom when you get to heaven,
little crimson rose!'
She met her end with that refrain:
'You're the one for me!'

                    June 16th 1919

[11]

She sat on everybody's knees,
had everybody's arms around her,
gave her love without reserve,
and when her eyes were looking at you,
God gazed down on you from Heaven.

June 16th 1919

TO ALYA

Above her blouse run through with silver threads –
as if the chest were stitched across with stars! –
her head is like the calyx to a flower,
emerging from the neckline worked in silver.

Two lakes on a heathland expanse, her eyes
carry the force of divine revelations –
Warfare and Inspiration have suffused
her lineaments with a vague, rosy haze.

An angel to whom nothing – everything! –
has been disclosed, to whom a blade of grass
is food enough, in you I see your father –
he, too, an angel and a warrior.

Maybe all I can do's aspire to stray
hand in hand with you from place to place.
Tomorrow morning, offer a prayer for
our fighters on the Kazan Virgin's feast!

July 5th 1919

You think: 'Sheer downright fraudulence, like soldiers
marching after each other in the barracks!
It doesn't matter no hint of a blush
can be traced on her high-flown, rosy lips –
rose seeds can be death-dealing, just the same!'
That's what you think: 'Sheer downright fraudulence!'

And you others, you ask: 'Why is it my
window she knocks on with that luminous finger?
She's fond of upstarts – I don't have a Kremlin!
Years have passed since my lover's pilgrimage
came to its end. My house is dark, deaf, silent.
My heart sleeps soundly beneath seven seals.'

And further: 'In a year when everyone
was orphaned, she took up her orphan's bag
and went from house to house, spreading a plague
of love, to demonstrate that she had power
over each [...] A devil in my house!'
And the answer I give? – 'Let it be thus!'

July 1919

THE GRANDMOTHER

I

When I get to be a granny
in a decade's time or so –
helterskelter, laugh a minute,
a whirlwind from top to toe! –

and my grandson, who'll be curly
and named Georgie, calls out for
a rifle, I'll cast pen and paper –
my whole treasure store – aside!

His mother will be howling: 'Barely
fifteen months old! What a menace!'
All I'll say's: 'Don't hold him back!
He's the image of his granny!

George, who came from my own entrails!
George, grown from a rib of mine!
George, my little Superman!
You'll beat them all and rule the world!'

When I get to be a granny,
a grey-haired hag who smokes a pipe,
at night my granddaughter will whisper,
creeping close, waving her skirts:

'I've got seven of them on
my heels, Granny! Which one to take?'
Knocking the bench over, I'll
start spinning round, like a whirlwind.

'Shameless! Senseless!' cries her mother.
'She'll dance her way into the grave!'
I'll wish the girl the best of luck:
'She's the image of her gran!

If he dances well at market,
darling, he'll be great in bed –
Marinushka, Marinushka,
Marina, blue as the sea!'

'Dearest Granny, now's the time to
say how many men you've kissed!'
'I paid all my debts with poems,
people paid me back in rings.

I didn't waste one night just sleeping,
spent them all in paradise!'
'OK Granny, tell us what
you'll tell God when he comes to judge?'

'Starlings chatter in the nest box,
spring brings the trees out in white . . .
Cousin,' I'll say, 'I'm a sinner!
I had a whale of a time!

As for you, ribs from my ribcage,
Marinushka, Rambo George,
make a fistful of whatever's
left behind of me on earth.'

July 23rd 1919

2

When finally the day arrived
on which granny would pop her clogs
what did her two lovie-dovie
offspring do but start to coo?

'What's up, old crock,
why the whingeing?'
Her answer came:
'What's with the cooing?'

'Our cooing is
your springtime song!'
'What makes me whinge
is sleep approaching,

eternal sleep
with lock and key,
for me, who partied,
never slept!

My meadows rich in eggs have not been scythed,
my merchant daughter's pearls have not been worn,
my forests filled with wolves have not been felled,
I've not loved my way through each Russian boy!'

Now granny was finally
breathing her last
her doves began beating
their wings on the window.

'Granny, what's making
your voice sound so awful?'
'I can't just hand over
the lads to the girls.'

'You had a load of fun –
time now for sense and shame!'
'And you, could you settle
for as little as this?

Me lying cold
next to this bonfire,
me sitting hungry
next to this table?'

When they arrived
to cart granny off,
all the doves did
was snuggle in bed:

little wings underneath,
paws on the top . . .
'Grandchildren, you're young – pray for your granny!'

July 25th 1919

▾   ▾   ▾

You won't succeed in driving me away!
Nobody's able to push spring aside!
You wouldn't dare so much as lay a finger
on me – my lullabies are far too tender!

You won't succeed in giving me a bad
name, for my name is water to the lips!
Nor will you succeed in leaving me:
the door stands open, your house is deserted!

July 1919

But on my forehead stars
– take note! – are burning.
In my right hand – heaven,
in my left hand – hell.

The silken belt I carry
wards off all afflictions.
My head reposes on
the book of Kingly Realms.

Many are like me
here in holy Russia –
you should ask the winds,
you should ask the wolves.

From one land to the next,
one city to the next,
In my right hand – heaven,
in my left hand – hell.

I gave you heaven mixed with hell to drink,
now your whole life is like one single day.

See me on my way,
bridegroom, for seven leagues!
Many are like me
here in holy Russia.

July 1919

To you, who should be born one hundred years
from now, so I get time to catch my breath,
out of my guts, like one condemned to die,
       I write, with my own fist:

Don't waste time looking for me! Fashions change!
Even the old men have forgotten me.
Our lips can't touch! Across Lethe's dark waters
       I stretch out both my hands.

I can see your eyes, a pair of bonfires,
blazing at me in the grave, in Hell,
fixed on a woman who can't lift an arm,
       dead for a century.

Clutched in my palm like a fistful of dust,
I see my poems! Meanwhile, you are scouring
the four winds for the house where I was born,
       or else in which I'll die.

How you look at the living, happy women
that cross your path fills me with pride – I catch
your words: 'Pack of impostors! You're all dead!
      She alone is alive!

I served her with a volunteer's devotion!
Knew all her secrets, where she hid each ring!
You're nothing but graverobbers! All the rings
      you wear you stole from her!'

I had a hundred! My whole body aches,
never before have I regretted handing
them out to right and left unthinkingly –
      couldn't I wait for you?

I'm saddened, too, that I spent a whole evening –
today's – in ceaseless pursuit of the setting
sun, in the hope of bumping into you
      across one hundred years.

I'd lay a wager you'll be hurling curses
upon my friends, hidden in the grave's gloom:
Much as you praised her, nobody would buy
      her the rose-coloured dress!

Was anyone less selfish?' No, I was
selfish. You cannot kill me, I won't hide
what I did – begged everyone for your letters
        to kiss them after dark.

Shall I say it? Here goes! No longer living's
a turn of phrase. You're my impassioned guest,
and you'll refuse the pearl among all women
        for the sake of my bones.

August 1919

I'd reached the point of shedding tears
saltier than salt, as women do
like her, on the grass, with a rake,
or her, in the field, with a sickle.

My voice had turned more faint than wax,
like sugar that's been dipped in tea.
Gripped in my teeth I brought the prey
to my marksman, a well-trained hound.

'You eat the kernel, as for me,
the walnut shell will keep me going.'
Nobody saw the treacherous
smile tug the corners of my mouth.

Those heroes of mine never guessed
the meek dove sticking by the holy
mountain's rules was like an emperor
in her unutterable pride.

August 1919

▼　　　▼　　　▼

Two trees long to reach each other,
two trees opposite my house.
The trees are old, the house is old.
I'm young and not, perhaps, inclined
to pity someone else's trees.

The lower one puts out its hands
like a woman racked in torment,
it's quite unbearable to see
how it strains towards the other,
older, sturdier and – who knows?
possibly still more unhappy.

Two trees: amidst the sunset dust,
beneath the rain, beneath the snow,
eternally, towards each other,
such is the law, the only law,
each of them towards the other.

August 1919

Consuela! Consolation! Don't
cast the evil eye on me, good people!
If God endowed me with a second shadow,
his bounty to me is unparalleled.

You cannot doubt it, I slept with an angel,
I must have had God himself in my arms.
Not an hour passes by without me blessing
the depths of night in which you were conceived.

Until the time set down for me arrives
my firstborn child, with eyes of palest blue,
will be my guide along a dust-white road
leading to God. Consolation! Consuela!

The life I had was so different before!
I was a woman everyone could envy!
They mounted a joint guard upon my house –
each hand had business underneath my pillow!

No way to tell what my reward would be:
from one, a smile and from the next, a farthing . . .
From time to time a man would go so far
as to leave me his heart beneath the pillow!

That was my golden age, I can't deny it!
I committed a host of glorious sins!
But then a snowstorm blew round me, and swept
you all away – Consuela – Consolation.

Nowadays I keep my attic clean,
scoop up the rubbish, toss it in the brazier.
Death may come to take us right away:
nobody has a crumb of love to offer!

Robber! Don't waste time! I won't be winkled
out! I'm going to sleep, as ordered by
one who can offer, against all the wrongs
they've done me, Consolation – Consuela!

October 1919

TO ALYA

I

In you there's not one drop of blood that's healthy.
You look as if your place were in a circus.

Observe her rising over the abyss,
exultant, scattering kisses everywhere,

smiling tensely, egging on the crowd
of plebeians applauding far below.

Your slender body looks entirely bloodless –
from head to toe, the novice we desired.

Little one, are you trembling at the knees?
Everything's as it ought to be: the rope –

the stretcher. And the spectacle your mother
laid on's dispelled in clouds of blue-grey incense.

October 1919

2

I never lift a finger when you fall.
I love you the same way I would a son.

Giving full satisfaction to my dream,
I spare you nothing, offer no compassion.

The lesson that I have for you is this:
lips can learn a lot from scalding iron.

More than from velvet carpets, youthful steps
learn what they need when forced to walk on nails.

And when the night is starless, best of all
if abysses can gape beneath the feet!

My firstborn with the stubborn brow!
Rather than what you'll learn from me,
better to have stayed on where
you were, inside your mother's womb.

October 1919

God! I'm alive! That means you aren't dead yet!
God, you and I can set up an alliance!
You, though, are a grumpy old man
and I'm a herald with his trumpet.

God! You can sleep at night in your blue heavens!
But as for me, among the living –
rely on me! My forehead meets the storms,
I am your armies' drummer-boy.

I blow your trumpet. I give out
the evening signal and the dawn reveille.
The love I feel for you is not
a daughter's, but a son's.

Flames cannot harm my soldier's tent.
Look at it! It could be the burning bush.
I wouldn't change my duties for a seraph's:
I'm God's own volunteer.

Just say the word and the Tsar-Maiden
will romp all through the villages!
Till then, let people take us for a songster
in an attic and a king of cards!

October 1919

Somebody walks behind a plough
rebuilding nests.
The only way of serving God:
look at the stars.

Feet rooted to the spot, you failed
to see my stars,
or else found more eternal ones –
thank you for that.

One fraud yields its place to the next,
Rachel to Lia.
Women are paths into the dark:
I'm like the rest.

October 1919

▼   ▼   ▼

Masks and music. What's the third
thing he loves? He won't say.
And I won't say either.

One thing, though, I know for sure –
I'd stake my crazy head on it! –
it's not his mother or his wife.

One thing, though, I know for sure –
like music and like masks,
Moscow, magnets, merriment,

mayhem and mazurkas,
its first letter is 'M'.

Could it be maypoles? Mandarins?

October 1919

My attic palace, my palatial attic!
Step along, by this heap of manuscripts . . .
Give me your hand. That's it! Keep to the right . . .
Avoid the puddle from the leaking roof.

Take a seat on the trunk, and then admire
the tapestry a spider wove for me.
Pay no attention to the idle talk
that claims women can get by without lace!

Start on your list of all our attic wonders:
angels and demons are our visitors,
plus one coming from somewhere higher still –
it's just a step from heaven to the roof!

Let me present my daughters – little attic
empresses – and then my cheerful muse –
they can show you round our Olympus, while
I heat a supper such as spectres eat.

I see you getting anxious. 'But how will
you manage? Who will bring the firewood up?'
Poets have fiery words to throw away!
Always! No danger we'll run out this year . . .

Poets have chewed hard crusts for centuries,
and we've no business with Bolshevik Moscow!
Just take a look, from one side to the other –
we've got our own Moscow – entirely blue!

If Moscow in the plague year takes too lively
an interest in the poet, there's an answer.
We're capable of doing without bread!
It's just a step from the roof – into heaven.

October 1919

I just can't get rid of you soon enough,
my carefree days of youth! Pig in a poke!
With one sweep of my hand, I'd put a cross
through all of you, beginning, middle, end!

I'd curl up snugly, deep in an armchair,
surrounded by the heavens' countless planets,
and put my young godsons and goddaughters
through the gallows university.

I'd show them how to light a fire, bake pizza,
gobble it down, then how to pull the wool
over a judge's eyes, how to betray
[…] their father and their mother.

Step over here one moment, little sparrow!
In that house they've a pearl big as a pea.
The pearl will […]
As for the sparrow – they can string him up!

All seven planets shine upon your path.
Blood must be shed to get you where you're going.

So set it flowing, do as you've been taught,
my little gallows sparrow, full of fun!

What's up with you? Tired sleeping with your husband?
Knock him down so he won't get up again,
and then contract a marriage with the winds!
Put yourself first! Your head must start to spin!

Meanwhile the spider [...] spinning its web:
'Red lips, white cheeks – now you're hunchbacked and bent,
everything's whirling round like a red dome,
make sure they wash you after you've been hanged!'

That's what I'll say from deep in my dark armchair,
surrounded by the heavens' countless planets
[...]
my godsons and goddaughters for the gallows.

Leaving his food, he sees the world's on fire,
[...] scorched earth half the way around.
'And granny?' 'Nobody knows where she's gone!
She fell out of her armchair into Hell!'

October 1919

There was a time when I was garlanded
with flowers, and poets composed stanzas to me.
The year nineteen nineteen's forgotten I'm
a woman . . . I've forgotten it myself!

They say my name – at once, as in a mirror
[...]
I could be an abandoned church. Above me
hang heavy clouds of pointless sympathy.

And so, buried alive in [...] Moscow,
I wander, a faint smile upon my lips.
After three years keeping out of my way,
these days you cross the road so we don't meet.

October 1919

You can decide: I've chopped up so much firewood
I can't tell if it's splitting, or my back.
The main thing is, I spoke no ill of you.
The main thing is, I kept my own good nature.

I've slaved away for peasants and old women
until I dropped – that throbbing at my temples!
It's high time you arrived to lend a hand –
after all, each of us has only two.

October 1919

S.E.

Want to know how my days proceed
here in the land where insults reign?
I use my hands to guide a saw,
meanwhile my heart utters a name.

All you would need to do is call
around – you'd realise! At night
I sing like I was sawing through
something quite different from wood.

Free until now, my hands can't get
past their surprise, holding a saw.
Our Lady of the Snowstorms sets
snowstorm on snowstorm hurtling past.

November 1919

We take the road of ordinary folk
without pretensions, folk who honour God,
not bound by ties, indifferent to fashion,
noble in our bodies and our souls.

The ancient prophecies have come to pass:
Where are you now, majesties, highnesses?

Mother and daughter on our pilgrimage,
mingling with the base and upstart mob,
maybe all we shall leave behind's a sigh,
maybe the Lord turns back to look at us . . .

Let whatever His will is be accomplished –
we aren't majesties or highnesses.

Without pretensions, honouring our God,
noble in our bodies and our souls,
we take the road of ordinary folk,
towards the country that is yours and mine:

towards a land of dreams and loneliness,
where we shall be majesties, highnesses.

1919

TO BALMONT

The roses in our cheeks are fading,
sumptuous and dispassionate.
Jackets buttoned up more tightly,
we're starving like they do in Spain.

We accept nothing free of charge –
moving mountains is easier!
On top of the old self-conceit,
hunger's a further cause for pride.

Turning our cloaks inside out,
the kind the people's enemies wear,
our way of walking shows we stand
by onion domes and liberty.

Life's carthorse pole will never break
the thoroughbred of arrogance.
No way to tell how this will end –
onion domes, and then the grave.

Beneath an almond tree, we'll have
our say when we reach heaven's gate:
Emperor! At the people's feast
we starved the way hidalgoes do!

November 1919

▼   ▼   ▼

My attic skylight up on high!
Your little ring can't reach that far!
Through the panes the sunlight lays
a cross upon the wall beneath,

faint shadow of the window frame.
Peace. Until the end of time,
giving me the feeling I've
been buried in heaven itself!

November 1919

TO ALYA

I

Sooner or later, creature of enchantment,
I shall become a memory for you,

lost amidst everything your pale blue eyes
have contemplated – continents apart.

You will forget the hooked nose of my profile,
my forehead with its cigarette smoke haloes,

my constant laughter, which fooled everyone,
the myriad rings upon my working woman's

fingers, and our attic like a cockpit,
the heavenly subversion of my papers . . .

the fearsome year when Want raised us aloft,
in which you were a child, and I was young.

2

Vagabond, with no memories of a family! –
Youth! – I remember: a blizzard of snow
in which the heart sang. From a sheltered room
I carried you outside into the storm.

[...]
And your voice, as the snowflakes whirled around:
'Mummy! Can you cut my hair off, please?
You see, it keeps me tethered to the earth!'

November 1919

3

Little spirit of the home,
presiding genius of my home!
Look at her, the place where two
related inspirations part!

It makes me sad when you can't see
the embers glowing in the stove!
Star of my night, you don't come through
the door, and you don't leave by it!

Your little clothes are hanging up
as if they were forbidden fruit.
A garden blossoms – to no point! –
just outside our attic window.

Pigeons knock against the pane –
what use are they as company?
The passing winds shout me their greeting –
what good is that? Winds, on your way!

They're colourless, and like the flocks
of pigeons, quite incapable
of saying, in the wonder-working
tones that you would use: 'Marina!'

November 1919

▾   ▾   ▾

Sitting in unlit carriages
or hanging on like death
to trembling, overcrowded footboards
with people who till yesterday were slaves,
I can't stop thinking about you, my son –
prince with the shaven head!

In the old days, you had your hair,
every strand of it so precious!

When love's a mere hair's breadth away,
even in anger […] nations can
be forged with one sole strand of a child's hair!
And in a hovel, on a makeshift bed,
prince with the shaven head.

My prince, my refugee!
Are you able to smile?
We've had far too much snow
this year!

Too much snow and too little bread.
Trembling footboards.

Kuntsevo, November 1919

The soul's immortal gift!
Pearl-like trace of a tear!
My wretched merchandise
of use to nobody!

Hearts count for nothing here! –
people are otherwise rich!
The writing on my wall:
too light-hearted by half!

December 19th 1919

I want neither to eat, nor drink, nor live.
Merely to fold my arms, while silently
my gaze surveys an untenanted skyline.
I neither care for freedom, nor deplore it,
dear God! I won't so much as lift a finger.
With folded arms, all I want's to stop breathing.

December 1919

I kissed him on the head without
thinking I could have kissed his lips!
Yet, raking through old memories,
I can recall your splendours, Love!

How good to drink plenty of cheering
wine and take one's fur coat off.
It revives from old memories,
the way my blood would start to beat!

Not any more – in such a year
love doesn't assume female form.
Axe in her hands, Venus smashes
the cellar into smithereens.

Caught in a Hell of plague and ice,
taking winter for his bride,
Eros has traded in his pair
of baby wings for padded boots.

Utterly enchanting creature!
A bit of smart abseiling – I
can still remember how it worked –
settle by the girl on her bed.

'That can't be done for some time yet!'
Before it happens, we'll acquire
old skills again, know better than
to kiss a young man on the head.

December 1919

FOUR-LINERS

I

My rings upon so many hands.
my songs upon so many lips,
my tears wetting so many eyes . . .
paraded through the squares – my youth!

2

Grandmothers love even the worst grand-daughters!
I took my torment by her little hand:
'One hundred nights, no sleep – unbearable!
Come for a walk, now – that might help you sleep!'

3

Battling to get out of passion's rut,
a day will dawn on which I'll say: 'No loving!'
Where, in the calendar of centuries
are you, though, day on which I'll say: 'No poems!'?

4

A drop fell on my eyes
like a warm tear.
High in heaven,
someone's crying for me.

5

All at once, while leafing through
my songs, I come upon – my soul.
Just for the record – no-one's tenant!
The house that's mine's yet to be built.

6

It'll happen tomorrow . . . The day after . . .
That's how Love keeps count on the first day.
But when the last day comes: If only all
of this had been a century ago!

7

The songbird always craves the grove
but, dallying with a speck of grain,
I lifted you out of the mud
where you were born – and put you back.

8

You tell me I'm a whore – and but
for one small detail, you are right:
I only accept handsome clients –
moreover, I don't let them pay.

9 FIVE-LINER

You're on – the two of us can play
and, what is more, with different styles;
you keep the rules, I swindle, but
however dishonest my game,
it's only me that stakes my life.

10

I bring you my heart like a bird
they've caught, with only one concern:
don't let the boys take it away,
don't let it struggle free itself!

11

But look, where tears are being shed,
entering I reconcile them all!
I'm an oriole, after rain
my voice is heard first in the wood.

12

In your homes everything's kept under
lock and key except for hearts.
All that's mine inside a house
is what's just asking to be taken.

13

I'm no rebel, I keep the rules. Whoever
steps across me to soar on high's a friend.
One thing, though, don't forget – taking yourself
in hand, you have released your hold on me.

14

Those entering the world clench small hands tight:
they're like aggressors, bent upon attack!
Those entering the earth have open palms –
all of our regiments got smashed to bits!

15

No need for shame, my Russian land!
Angels have always gone barefoot . . .
Boots are footwear for the devil.
Now who's shod is to be feared!

[16]

While your eyes follow me into the grave,
write up the whole caboodle on my cross!
'Her days began with songs, ended in tears,
but when she died, she split her sides with laughter!'

[17]

All at once, while leafing through
my songs, I come upon – my soul.
But I'm a perilous intruder:
I'll take the whole house off with me.

[18]

You brought me a fistful of rubies,
but I love lips like roses more.
I won't say no to millions offered,
but I can't be bought with roubles.

[19]

You tell me I'm a whore – you're right.
But one thing you must not forget:
I'd rather huddle by the stove
than give a single kiss to you.

[20]

You tell me I'm a whore – but listen,
you with those degrees of yours:
first, my clients must be civil,
second, time for you to go.

[21]

There was a robbery in your house
but I'm not the guilty one.
All that's mine inside a house
is what's just asking to be taken.

[22]

Clatter of steps outside the window.
No idea what time it is.
God's Mother be your saviour when
you count steps passing by at night!

[23]

A step outside the door.
Again, no need to worry.
Of one thing there's no doubt:
soon a new step will sound.

[24]

An entry in the guest book:
'I went out empty-handed.'
From a professional thief –
be thankful for small mercies.

1919–1920

Between Sunday and Saturday
I hung, bird at an Easter fair,
one of my wings was coloured silver,
the other wing was coloured gold.

Divided in two, half of me
high-spirited, and half afflicted,
my silver part was Saturday,
but Sunday was the gold in me!

Aching sadness filled my veins,
crumbs could offer no delight.
You have to know, from my right wing
I let a feather fall, a quill.

My blood came back to life again,
I brought the feather to my cheeks –
in other words, the side I turned
to the world was my golden one.

Enjoy me while you can! For soon
your bird of varied feathers will
disappear to far-off climes,
your Easter bird flaked silver, gold.

December 29th 1919

A rose of flame in the blue sky:
a heart's been sewn onto the banner.
Onwards, kin to nobody,
the youthful standard-bearer strides.

A garden flower in the blue field:
that's the place where he's at home.
The standard-bearer has no other,
him there, with the flaxen hair.

Standard-bearer, standard-bearer,
why should you bring our enemy
a red flower into the blue field?

After his chest had been pierced through
they wrapped his body in his banner.
One heart upon another heart.

That's his home now. That's the only
home the standard-bearer has.

December 29th 1919

▼   ▼   ▼

Pardon Love! Begging through the streets,
she wears shoes that are caked in dirt,
that is, if she has shoes at all!

Last night I found her praying to
God's Mother outside the church porch
and let her have one of my shoes.

I gave street kids the other one
on the corner by the baker's,
where the man I loved would pass.

Now I'm barefoot, like the angels!
Love doesn't know how comfortable
the shoes waiting in heaven are.

December 30th 1919, Kuntsevo – hospital

▾   ▾   ▾

A star above the cradle, and one more above the grave!
Stretched between them, like a pale blue snowdrift,
the whole of life. – But then, I am your mother,
There's nothing more that I can say to you,
my star! . . .

January 4th 1920, Kuntsevo – hospital

Born of debauch and separation,
I stretch my hands towards everyone.

Eyelashes fluttering, I tug
the edge of all the young men's coats.

A voice sounds: Mariula, go!
And I push everyone away.

January 1920

▼　　▼　　▼

Getting your way thanks to a coach
and a guitar means not a single
woman can resist you, means you
circle like vintage ale from head
to head! Adonis! And a halfblood!
Who christened you? And in what font?
Every gypsy snowstorm set your
jerkin flapping, virtuoso!
I fear the pitted roads and your
guitar strings can lay me flat out!
God be with you, coachman Sergey!
I'm a woman, same as Russia!

January 1920

My first grandmother bore four sons,
four sons, four chips off the same block,

sheepskin jacket, hemp rucksack,
four sons – but just one pair of hands!

You keep filling their bowls – they're empty!
No nobleman's sons! Make them priests!

The other was so different! All
Poland's gentry groaned at her feet.

See her laughing by the fire:
'Hundreds worship – just one hand!'

Cavorting with those much kissed hands
across the keyboard, clothed in silk . . .

They're both in me, the one who did
slave labour, the one with white hands!

January 1920

I'll let the wind transport this book,
it and the cranes it comes upon.
Long since I tore my vocal chords
drowning separation out.

A bottle in the waves, I toss it
into the whirlwind of war.
Let it wander, like a feast day
candle, passed from hand to hand.

Wind, wind, my trustworthy witness,
take it to the ones I love,
proceeding, even in their sleep,
night after night from north to south.

February 1920

You've travelled a long way, sleep sound in your new cell!
No problem if you dream about the world you left
behind, the coats of arms, the epaulettes.
We can have all the fun we want, thinking
of that which we once were, and are no more!

A valet spreads the travelling rug out.
The punch is fiery and, in retrospect,
the ballet's a snowstorm of darting roses.

For every single petal, may you have
a year of revels, luxury and
indolence, my foreigner, my neighbour!

Beginning of March 1920

Punch and midnight. Punch – and Pushkin.
Punch, puffs at a foaming pipe.
Punch – tapping of dancing shoes
on creaking floorboards. And – a ghost! –
beneath the arch's crescent – like
a bird, a night-time butterfly – Psyche!
'Not sleeping yet?' she whispers. 'I
wanted to say goodbye . . .' Her eyes
are downcast. (Is she seeking advance
pardon for the pranks in store
that night?) Each finger of the tiny
hands alighting on your shoulder,
each pearl on the soft, pliant neck
has been kissed one hundred times.
Standing on tiptoe – a peri! –
pirouetting – a mirage! –
she's darted off.
                            Punch – and midnight.
She flutters in once more: 'I'm so
forgetful! What about my fan?
Now I'll be late . . . The first round of
the polonaise . . .'

                His greatcoat thrown
across one shoulder, the obedient
poet takes her hand, and shows
Psyche the way down the trembling
staircase. Carefully he tucks
the she-wolf's paws into the plaid
and wraps her in the fur . . . 'Goodbye!'

                          But Psyche
huddles close to her companion
– blind scarecrow in a cap. She's trembling:
perhaps the kisses of that rogue
have burned a hole into her glove . . .

              ˅   ˅   ˅

Punch and midnight. Punch and ashes
falling on the Persian robe
colour of straw – a ballroom dress's
empty foaming
in the dusty mirror . . .

                          Beginning of March 1920

▼   ▼   ▼

His gown is coloured raspberry
and turquoise, and he wears a ring
as talisman. A clouded gaze,
lost somewhere underneath the lids,

sluggishly follows every puff
from his rose-coloured crystal pipe.
Skirts spread open the way a rose
opens its bloom, sheltering beneath

his gown's two flaps, leaning against
his shoulders, like two snakes, two girls
wearing necklaces bend over,
concentrating on a chessboard.

The flap colour of raspberries
hides one, the turquoise flap the other.
Their eyes are lowered. Not a word's
said, while their eyelashes wage war.

Now and again, a serpent's tail,
a patterned stocking toe peeps out
from underneath the players' peacock
skirts – no more. He is at stake.

The game proceeds relentlessly.
He smokes. He has a childish grin.
The moon, a scimitar, hatches
plots within the palace window.

March 19th 1920

She creeps up imperceptibly,
like midnight in the trembling wood.
I know it's doves I'm bringing you,
wrapped in my sumptuous pinafore.

No way to shift me from the door!
Shame pins me down, weighty as lead.
But doves get tired of pinafores –
it flies off without asking leave!

March 19th 1920

OLD-FASHIONED DEFERENCE

Tenderly, two hands repulse
his angelic rascalry.
Next he's resting at her feet,
strumming the strings of his lute.

Melodious whisperings from the cistern,
avowal in a bowl of flowers,
faced with a springtime shyness, where
are you, old-fashioned deference?

Window where a light burns long
while the streetlamp grows more feeble . . .
A sigh as duty triumphs, an
'I can't' that can't be argued with.

Wreathed in autumn mist, a courteous
hand gestures just one last time.
Faced with a muslin fortress, where
are you, old-fashioned deference?

His letters are brief . . . and infrequent . . .
She, a Psyche, bodiless,
reads verses from *Ecclesiastes*,
not opening the *Song of Songs*.

The song's unchanged, no doubting that.
But, bent over the family Bible,
(God is my whole estate), where are
you now, old-fashioned deference?

March 19th – April 2nd 1920

▼　　▼　　▼

Equally young, equally ragged,
sharing nights around the bonfire . . .
This heaven-inspired lyre of mine
is the sister of your guitar.

Fate assigned us the same gift
of circling, a snowstorm, through souls.
I was still an infant when
they christened me robber of souls.

Wringing your hands in agony,
remember that you're not the only
one who sets princes' heads reeling
with the gypsy broth of parting.

When, faced with a knife blade, the blood
pumps faster through your veins, remember
you're not alone. We're sisters in
the great abasement that is love.

March 1920

Do I love you?
I thought it through.
Meanwhile my two eyes got bigger.

Forest river,
a stubborn hand
entangled itself in my curls.

Love's out of date.
I chew my pen.
I'm too lazy to light a candle.

There'll be a tale!
That's the reason
you're born into this world a poet!

I lent it, then
I took it back.
(It's dark, and my pen's working hard.)

Let's sort it out.
An equals sign
between love and goodbye to you.

Passion's been done.
Passion to write!
Suddenly roses fill the house!

Some fragrances
are like commands.
I lean my forehead on my hand.

Palm Sunday
March 22nd 1920

From seven until seven
we finished the removal.
We had great fun and laughter
from seven until seven!

What happens when young people
face each other in a dark
garret? (Don't keep me waiting!
Quick! I want an answer!)

Nothing quite so outrageous
happened with us (we've still
got time!) Hearts were united,
hands stayed in different places!

Leaning over the cradle
he kept clear of two heads –
I was safe. We shared our bread,
but not a bed, at midnight.

Those night shifts were like heaven
on loan! They're over now.
The coming nights will be
blameless, though filled with love!

Making a garret home –
from seven until seven
no […] or embraces –
fun stayed within the rules
from seven until seven!

March 1920

▼   ▼   ▼

'I've sunk so low, and you're so wretched,
so isolated and alone.
Both of us sold for a farthing
despite our good characters . . .

I don't own so much as a stick . . .'
She used the note to light the stove . . .

Palm Sunday 1920

▾　　▾　　▾

You'd take him for an emperor's son.
– But why? – He's just far too good-looking.
He can't be someone ordinary.

The seven-year-old blurts it out,
next the older one gives a sigh . . .
But both are fools. Can you expect

common sense from such bright eyes?
Both read their fill of fairy tales –
for them, night is the same as day.

Our advice to the emperor's son
wearing a jerkin? He should stroke
the seven-year-old's head, and then

her mother's, each taking a turn.
[...]
Or why not stroke them both at once?

March 1920

▼　　▼　　▼

Dying, I'll regret the gypsy songs.
Dying, I'll regret my [...] rings,
cigarette smoke, sleeplessness, a flock
of weightless verses underneath my hand.

My wretched works, that tower of Babylon;
a smouldering pile of letters, mine and others' . . .
Cigarette smoke, sleeplessness, foreheads,
light and rebellious, resting on my hand.

3rd day of Easter 1920

BALLAD OF THE OUTCAST GIRL

When I was a tiny thing,
half-crazy, barely clothed,
thank God, I wasn't one to hang
onto my mother's skirts.

I vaulted bars and palisades,
wrecked gardens and forged hooves!
At night, where unknown people lived –
Give me somewhere to sleep!

I grew as straight as arrows fly.
All at once evening fell,
black as pitch, I found a vagrant
fiddler underneath an oak.

[...] were sleeping, flowers and bees . . .
What name to give to this?
I overcame a woman's shame –
Give me somewhere to sleep!

I never closed an eye at night!
We did it every way!
[...] Who wasn't called
to my school of perdition?

You're barely wrapped in your greatcoat
and there I stand, in rags.
Like a hammer on your brow:
Give me somewhere to sleep!

Envoi
Angels surrounding the high throne
and you, Mother so young!
I've had enough of revelling –
Give me somewhere to sleep!

April 2nd 1920

AFTER H. HEINE

Here is a sign for you, like it or not!
Our battle's not over – it's hardly begun!
That's how it went in the life we have here:
the guy ends up singing, his girlfriend in tears.

I can't wait to see – in the life that's to come,
I'll do the singing and you'll be in tears!

Bell in the hand!
Imp in the blood!
Crimson red skirt!
Hearts black as pitch!

My skirt is so red it sets heaven on fire!
Like a carpet for me, your young homage spread out!
I'll treat you the way people treat butterflies!
But as goes for you, you'll treat me like a sailor!

Crimson red skirt? What else did you expect?
Fire-coloured sail! A beacon bright red!

Bell in the hand!
Imp in the blood!
Crimson red skirt!
Hearts black as pitch!

How will you know me? Skin white as chalk,
no hint of laughter, but my lips will move.
If what you want's to get burned, as you've seen,
remember I'm going to come back with red hair.

Red as the leaf on that maple tree there,
red like the one you see hang in the woods.

Bell in the hand!
Imp in the blood!
Crimson red skirt!
Hearts black as pitch!

Beginning of April 1920

▾   ▾   ▾

But when I come again into this world
where I bestow on everyone my verse,
my ear, I will be deaf and dumb. No matter what

they say, I cannot understand a word,
nor can they understand a thing I say.

May God preserve me! Returning, a second
Corinna, to this land where men are harder
than ice, and ice-floes than a cliff! My pony-tail

reaching down to the floor, and deaf and dumb,
so there's no danger I'll be recognised!

April 7th 1920

Two hands, each lowered gently
onto a young child's head!
I was given two of them,
one beneath each hand.

Using both, clenched tight
and fiercely as I could,
I snatched the older from the dark
but lost the younger one.

Two hands to fondle and caress
those fluffy, tender heads.
Two hands – within a single night
I had no use for one.

Bright, upon its slender neck,
a dandelion stalk!
It's still impossible to grasp
my child lies in the earth.

Easter Monday 1920

A SON

Left arm akimbo, one foot poised
for your next step – this is the pose
you assume. In your eyes a steely
glitter. No hint of a smile.

Redder lips and blacker brows
can be found. But that colouring!
Sunlight's less bright! The hour's not struck
for the shears to trim that shearling.

All women want to kiss your hands,
forgetting they've sons of their own.
A tensed string! In your beauty there's
no trace of the world-weary Slav.

Such brilliance turns me to a pillar.
I know my last hour is at hand!
Accomplishing the poem, what
else can the poet do but die?

Emerging from the watchful shadows
of the Kremlin's topmost towers,
in the twilight throng I glimpsed
one who's still to arrive – *my son.*

Easter Monday 1920

TO VYACHESLAV IVANOV

I

Your finger's writing in the sand.
But I've arrived, and start to read.
The hair is greying at your temples.
As for me – my hair's still gold.

Eyes filled with life have buried me
as if it were in a sand dune.
That's how children bend bright brows
over a Bible the first time.

I'd rather break up stones, or be
a dove lost in a flock of crows!
Night covers every grain of sand,
I can't stop reading, I'm still here.

2

Your finger's writing in the sand.
Rabbi, I am your turtle-dove!
I'm the firstborn on your list
of good wishes and memories.

I set my necklace tinkling so
you'll look around – but you don't hear!
Rabbi, Rabbi, I'm afraid –
I'm reading what you didn't write!

Like a thief, twilight steals close,
or like a fateful warrior band.
Rabbi, you get it, so I can
read better, I'm closing my eyes . . .

Your finger's writing in the sand . . .

Easter 1920

3

A favourite, not a paramour,
I set foot on this gentle earth.
Sobbing doesn't lie behind
the lifting of my boyish chest.

That's why I feel such tenderness –
not sighing and not languishing –
sitting on the little crimson
bench that's placed next to your feet.

Should I press my lips against
your drooping hand – don't think of frowning!
Admiring is my daily bread:
my lips are moving in a prayer.

Dearer to me than golden curls,
the tender hoarfrost creeping, inch
by inch, across the little crimson
bench that's placed next to your feet.

Burying my head in your
indulgent knees, I ask myself
if all the roses in the garden
have been gathered for your sake?

This I swear to: every single
heir to the throne lost his chance
of sitting on the little crimson
bench that's placed next to your feet.

I was singing songs, meantime
you dropped off – what more could I ask?
Most hallowed among all my tasks,
to keep watch over sleeping eyes.

If you could know how blessedly
I draw each breath – don't dare to sigh! –
here upon the little crimson
bench that's placed next to your feet!

First Sunday after Easter 1920

TO N(IKOLAY) N(IKOLAYEVICH) V(YSHESLAVTSEV)

Do not allow your passions to
overstep the limits of your will.
– But Allah is wiser . . .

Thousand and One Nights

I

Along great, silent roads,
taking great, silent strides . . .
Stone cast into water, the soul
sends out ever-widening ripples.

How deep that water is, how dark!
How much I want to reach the soul
buried eternally inside
and tell it: Enter into me!

April 27th 1920

2

All of the sea needs all of the sky,
all of the heart needs all of God.

April 27th 1920

3

"And nonetheless – that's England . . ."

Odour of England – of the sea –
of gallantry. Severe, proportioned.
Enmeshing myself in fresh pain,
I risk my way, like a ship's boy,

along a rope at the storm's height,
confronted with the Lord's anger.
Divinely foolish, like a monkey
I dance above those foaming jaws.

My grip is dogged, the rope holds,
this isn't the first storm it's seen!
My heart is stalwart – after all,
not everyone dies in his bed!

Watch as, at the mast's furthest tip,
I gulp in the chill, starless dark,
suspended on a gaping chasm –
laughing aloud! – and shut my eyes . . .

April 27th 1920

4

All we have's one hour of time
and then eternity apart!
Meantime in the hourglass the sand
trickles fast!

What it is in you attracts me
is of no credit to you!
Simply fear the flush may fade
from your cheeks.

Did you get familiarised
with time on convent garden sundials?
Did you weigh it on the scales
of heaven?

From thousands, one hour is assigned
to us, and to the constellations.
I'm determined not to let it
ebb away!

All I could steal, one meagre little
hour out of eternity.
One hour for [...] love from start
to finish.

I take the blame, I'll pay the price.
After which, the sand will cover
both of us.

5

"In this darkness I can't tell
what's hand, what's plank . . ."

A friend eyes have not seen, ears have not heard
is standing by your side. Put out the light!
I know all of the routes into and out
of this, the prison fortress of the soul.

The guards are all got up in crowns of roses –
that bunch of halfwits can't see past their hands!
A woman, I could blind them every one –
being blind, I'm able to see everything.

Shut your eyes. Do exactly as I say.
Give me your hand to hold. – The bolt's been drawn. –
Dawn's far away – those aren't clouds – my horse
is waiting till we get into the saddle.

Act like a man. I'll be your shield, your valour,
your passion, too, as I was in the past.
And if you feel your head begin to spin,
just lift your gaze towards the starry sky!

April 27th 1920

6

"Thing is, you never pass my house."

My way doesn't lead past your house.
My way leads past nobody's house.

And yet I keep going astray
(especially in spring),
can't help yearning for company, like
a dog beneath the moon.

Welcome in everybody's home,
I let nobody sleep!
Play dominoes with grandad, sing
songs with his grandson.

I don't make women jealous – I'm
merely a voice, a glance.
I never had a lover build
mansions just for me.

I burst out laughing at the pointless
hoards you amass, merchants!
I raise up palaces and bridges
in a single night.

(Pay no attention to my words!
They're woman's babbling!)
When morning dawns, with my own hands
I tear down what I built.

Like scattering straw, the mansion's gone!
My way doesn't lead past your house.

May 14th 1920

7

Sympathy in my neighbour's eyes,
the older woman's pace is measured.
Their dangling arms, like branches, are
indifferent as a god's might be.

The young man on his soapbox has
run out of steam and thunderbolts.
Fewer and fewer words fall on
my young forehead like weighty drops.

The moonlight runs along our limbs
in woollen tatters, just like smoke.
I love how it illuminates
our mutual indifference.

April 29th 1920

8

"Day is for working, evening for talking –
at night, we need to sleep."

I'd sooner give my life than sacrifice
an hour of this divine obscurity!
Go to bed early and get up at dawn –
that's the one order you have ever issued!

The thing is, even when I close my eyes
I have no certainty that dreams will come.
Might it not make things much simpler if
I used my own two hands for closing them?

I'm worried they'll stay open in the grave –
I'll be denied the sound sleep of the just.
Stop trying to change me. Owlets need the night,
and sleepless people need their sleeplessness.

May 16th 1920

9

Bagged and under water – that's real courage!
Stinginess in love's a greater sin.
Not harming the least hair upon my head,
you're anything but kindly to my soul.

Red domes are irresistibly attractive
to ravens and pigeons. Capriciousness
is as forgivable in curly heads
as winding tendrils are in hyacinths.

Hovering around a golden dome's
a sin if you don't say a prayer beneath.
Yet you don't show the slightest interest in
the soul that's hidden by this cap of curls!

However much time you spend contemplating
my golden locks, you miss the rueful protest:
How would it be if you paid half as much
attention to the wonders of my soul?

May 14th 1920

10

So trivial, so frivolous
you waste no scornful word on me,
if you are made from stone, I sing,
if you're a monument, I fly.

Seen from eternity, the charms
of May amount to nothing. But
I am a bird. Do not protest
if my law is a weightless one.

May 14th 1920

II

Repulsed by a blow to the chest –
trust to your legs! They'll keep you upright!
Then knock on someone else's door
for renewed evenings of deceit.

[...] from high on your tightrope
shower them with pearls and roses.
[...] what your friends need
is verses, not straightforward tears.

May 16th 1920

12

Having bid all passions farewell
you, too, forgive.
I've swallowed all the slights I could.
They're in your eyes, like a whip's lash,
the Bible's words:
'Passion's a sin!'

When my hands bring you food to eat,
you see – a crush.
Every heart envies my laughter –
to you it sounds
like lepers' bells.

To avoid taking mine, at once
your hands take hold of the pick-axe
(but don't both tasks end up in flowers?)
My eyes grow dark – it's obvious
among the sheep you tended none
was ever black.

But, thank God, an island exists
where I'll have no need of a bell,
where black fluff can
be gathered along every fence.
Flocks of just black sheep exist, with
different shepherds.

May 17th 1920

13

You've no end of complaints at my behaviour!
But maybe I prefer to be accursed!
It could well be the gypsy tatters that
I'm wrapped so humbly in

are just as precious as pure gold, glitter
as dazzlingly as an armoured knight
arraigned before a court!

The dancer mustn't tremble on his tightrope,
mustn't remember that he ever knew
another element

than air extending below his winged feet!
Don't interfere when, like you, he broadcasts
the tidings of his lord.

May 17th 1920

14

Don't hurry to reach a judgement!
Earthly judgements rarely last!
Don't slander the fledgling jackdaw's
dovelike candour! Who can tell,

persistence may pay off, and if
I love my way through everyone,
on that blackest of days I might
even wake up whiter than you!

May 17th 1920

[14a]

And yet for half an hour we two
were the very best of friends!
Who's to blame I wasn't born
different from the way I am?

Our common fate to leap into
paradise head over heels.
There they'll decide which was worth more:
my circus, or your sailor's rope.

15

"I neither want to offend you,
nor can, nor could."

When it's unbearable – the pain a woman
looks back on, the thirst, the passion – you,
in other words! – I rush out, so as to
forget – a towering ocean breaker, rolling

its foam past citizens, bags, bayonets,
down stony Soviet Povarskaya Street.

I bend over a tremulous Afghan hound –
and all at once his eyes are yours – the hands
on the icons are yours, if only you
had neither eyes nor hands to be remembered!

Homes are a crossword puzzle I can't solve
so take by storm, an ocean breaker playing.

I give kisses to everyone in turn.
Where I sit on the window-sill, Moscow's

spread out before me. All of it loves me!
There's where you live . . . Laughter comes, through clenched teeth.

My five-year old, having chewed all her millet,
says: 'When you go, we're bored. With you, it's fun . . .'

Set in a daisy chain of sleeping children,
I'm reached by drowsy words: 'They're hacking at
a tree's roots. Scary. A Pole. Any news?'
'No. Well, actually, yes. He doesn't love me!'

Astonishing her husband with my answer,
I call upon his wife to see how jealous

my friend is. Everyone gives flowers as payment
for my poems. A blizzard fills my arms!
My shadow flits from wall to wall. Onwards,
hoping that humanity's circus ring

can help me put grim memory to flight.
The worst thing would be coming to my senses!

Avoiding you as if you were the plague
I tour the city on long [dancer's] legs,
circling, circling, circling till night falls,
till finally I pause upon my own

doorstep, just long enough to catch my breath,
then enter. Who's waiting inside but you!

May 17th – 19th 1920

16

Filled with wonder, totally enraptured,
a daylight visionary, everyone
is used to seeing me with bleary eyes,
but nobody has ever seen me sleepy.

Given that from daybreak until nightfall
dreams float uninterrupted past my eyes,
I fail to see the point in going to bed.
It makes more sense, a melancholy shade,
to watch over the slumbers of my friends.

May 17th – 19th 1920

17

Nailed to the pillar of shame of my old
Slavic conscience, a snake in my heart, on
my forehead a brand, I declare that I'm
innocent, declare the peace I enjoy is

the same the communicant feels at the
sacrament. I can't be blamed if I stretch
out my hand in the squares for whatever
they're willing to give me. Try rummaging

through everything I possess – am I blind?
Can you see any gold, any silver?
I clutch in my fist nothing more than a
handful of ashes. Despite all my fawning

and pleading, I managed to get only
this out of people who're happier than me.
It's the luggage I'll take on departing
for the land where all kissing is wordless.

18

Even though nailed to the pillar of shame,
I keep declaring doggedly: I love you.

A woman who is mother to the core
doesn't give her child the looks you get.
You're too absorbed to notice I'd be willing
not just to die, but keep on dying for you.
Talking gets me nowhere, you can't grasp
the pillar of shame's no cause of shame to me!

If a regiment gave me its banner to carry
and suddenly you appeared before my eyes
bearing another, I'd turn to a pillar
of stone, my fingers slackening their hold . . .
Having managed this ultimate homage,
I'd collapse on the grass at your feet.

Given yours were the hands that nailed me there,
as far as I'm concerned, the pillar's turned

into a birch tree in a grove where armies
don't thunder, but doves coo at break of dawn . . .
I've given up so much, I won't relinquish
this black pillar for Rouen's fiery halo!

19

This is what you wanted. – Yes. – So be it.
I kiss the hand delivering the blow.

It rejects me, but I clutch it to me
so you can hear, and wonder at, the silence,

and then observe, with an indifferent grimace:
'At last my child is learning to obey!'

This didn't begin yesterday. I've been
clutching your monkish hand for centuries,

so cold it feels white-hot. Oh, Eloise!
The hand of your beloved Abelard.

In the pealing cathedral, may the lightning
white lashes of your whip scourge me to death!

May 19th 1920, Vigil of the Ascension

20

With this my hand, whose praises seafarers
have trumpeted one hundred leagues around,
forger of odes when darkness falls, I draw
a feeble cross, as if illiterate.

If that seems insufficient, then I'm willing
to set both of them on the block, unleashing
night after night, a joyous, blood-red wave
that can submerge these rivers of black ink!

May 20th 1920

21

If stanzas cannot help, nor constellations,
then this must be what's known as retribution
because, time and again,

straightening up over an awkward line,
above my forehead's spaciousness I looked
for stars only, not eyes;

because, acknowledging your suzerainty,
not for a single moment, gorgeous Eros,
did I accept your absence

when, in the ritual darknesses of night,
my booty, from a crimson, yielding mouth
was rhymes only, not lips;

because, though harshly judged, white as the snowy
skin beneath this left breast, I attained
the status of a god

and, face to face with the young Orient
in person, sought, above my forehead's breadth
daybreak, and not a rose!

May 20th 1920

22

You cannot do your dirty work quite so
straightforwardly, and then fall fast asleep.
Go on your way. High above, from the scaffold,
I nod to you once more.

You raise your eyebrows in astonishment,
realising your slanders had no point:
I did not write these words in purple ink –
but in dark, congealed blood.

23

Some are made of stone, and some of clay
but glittering silver is my element!
Named Marina, I'm set on betrayal,
the foam that teeters on the wave's poised crest!

Some are made of clay, and some of flesh,
such as the gravestone and what lies beneath –
baptized in the sea's font, when I take flight
I'm broken into fragments ceaselessly!

Subservient to none other than my will,
I drench each heart, each net I come upon.
Can you see these ungovernable curls?
You'll never extract earthbound salt from them.

Shattered on the granite of your knees,
wave after wave summons me back to life!
Accept this greeting from the joyous froth,
the foam that teeters on the wave's poised crest!

May 23rd 1920

24

Just take it all, I don't need any of it.
Place it safely in [...]
as once God, with his own hand, placed this blossom
beyond the lattice of a rose garden.

Just take all of the things I didn't buy:
my [...], my [...] and my notebook.
The mountain I fell down from was so high
life's never going to pick me up again!

I won't deny that right now I regret
having lived so ingloriously, so fast
asleep, like a blind puppy! You're doing me
a favour, thrusting me into the gutter.

Instead of all that might have been, [...],
the thundering waves of squares throughout the world,
you can acquire some puny credit seeing
after you [...] – another mound.

May 23rd 1920

25 DEATH OF THE DANCING GIRL

Beneath me the reception hall's
awash with glittering silk and white.
Inspiring terror, a black path's
the only way to you, alcove.

Upon their heads – warriors' helmets.
I see a fan, the rope, and in
your eyes a glazed expression, which
reflects the setting sun's last rays.

May 24th 1920

26

I've not been dancing, so I'm not to blame
if my rose-coloured dress starts billowing.
My two hands can outwit, quick as a flash,
the gust, imprison it and smooth things out.

Cunning, it gives no sign of life. But there
below the knees, the hem starts quivering.
I wish I could control this piece of madness
as easily as I do my billowing dress!

May 24th 1920

27

With the eyes of a witch under a spell
I gaze upon God's child, forbidden fruit.
Now they have endowed me with a soul,
silence and meekness are my sole resource.

Forgetting how, from dusk to dawn, I moaned,
a river seagull, under people's windows,
I go about my chores, blue-eyed, sedate
in a starched cap, the way a housewife does.

Even my rings have lost their fatal gleam.
My hand in the sunlight's a shrouded corpse.
My bread's so salty I can't swallow it,
the salt in the salt-cellar lies untouched . . .

May 25th 1920

My humble roof! Smoke from a beggar's fire!
So different from what I was born into!

From the window at which, incandescent,
we glowed, from the straightforward evening kiss
shunning the lips, somewhere along the cheek . . .

The day comes to a close, the bolt's in place:
now night, unvisited by love or dreams!

Night such as worn-out women reapers have
who work, with dogged souls and dogged bones,

from the time the dawn birds start to sing
so their children can get something to eat.

Oh, but to know for sure that, when the snow's
piled high, there will be flowers on my grave . . .

May 14th 1920

to S.E.

Here I sit, bereft of light, and bread,
and water. God
visits me with such misfortunes
he must plan to take me into
Heaven alive as reward for my pains.

Not a crust of bread has passed my lips
since morning. The dream tantalising me,
my warrior, though, is, I'll be so obedient
it'll be enough to win you back.

May 16th 1920

to S.E.

I wrote it on a blackboard of dark slate,
along the tiny folds of faded fans,
along a river's sands, on the seashore,
with skates on ice, using my ring on glass . . .

on treetrunks living a centennial winter
and, finally, so everyone can know
how constantly, unfailingly I love you,
added my name, a rainbow, on the sky.

How I yearned for each of them to flower
under my fingers, through the centuries
and then, resting my forehead on the table,
put crosses slantwise through all of the names . . .

And nonetheless some money-grubbing scribe
has got his hands on you, my whole heartache,
whom I never betrayed, escaping into
history on my ring's inner edge.

May 18th 1920

▾   ▾   ▾

Shadows have overtaken half a house
where nobody knows anything of me.
I'm not going to set pangs of love beside
the way a working day ennobles one.

Even an emperor can wear a crown
of this kind . . . Sweat upon a sovereign's brow!
And God will make a gift to me of sleep
in an unnamed, yet honourable grave.

May 21st 1920

▼   ▼   ▼

My pity goes to everyone!
To beggars and to emperors,
to the son, his father too . . .

The shadow there'll be on a face,
the one a future garland casts,
or from a sapling, paper-thin . . .

– And shoulders flop . . .

May 21st 1920

The women cried hurray
and threw their caps into the air.

I place my hand upon my heart and swear:
I'm not a lady of exalted rank!
My forehead's as rebellious as my womb.

Each random passer-by, each single square
can tell you of the riddles and the knots
like blemishes upon my family tree.

Kremlin! The same blackness is yours and mine!
Yet I acknowledge I rate Grishka's ashes
higher than those of anyone in power!

If I throw my cap into the air
what makes me different from a thousand lads
calling out from each square in the world?

So three cheers for the emperor, then! Three cheers
for all the royal arrivals on exultant
mornings, since the day the world began!

My soaring cap flies up beyond the towers,
passes the wrought iron garland circling
an idol's temples and reaches the stars!

May 21st 1920

▼   ▼   ▼

Half of the window has been opened.
Half of the soul has been revealed.
Why not open the other half
too, the remainder of the window?

May 25th 1920

Afterword

The Bolshevik coup on October 25th 1917 (Old Style) found Marina Tsve-
taeva far south, in the Crimea. Her husband was involved in street fighting
in Moscow, and came close to losing his life. She travelled for three days
and two nights in a crowded train, surrounded by increasingly terrifying
rumours, before reaching her native city, soon to be declared capital of the
new Russia. Tsvetaeva had seen the Tsar's abdication the previous spring as
a dereliction of duty. Her reaction to the latest turn of events could only be
wholesale rejection.

She once observed that she and her younger sister Anastasia (Asya) could,
if they wished, have been ladies-in-waiting at court. Marina Tsvetaeva was
born into a privileged background. Circumstances conspired to render it
equally unconventional. Her mother's death from tuberculosis in 1906, and
her father's preoccupation with setting up a major museum, left their chil-
dren practically without supervision. In summer 1909, aged sixteen, Tsve-
taeva travelled alone to Paris, where she took a room in Rue Bonaparte,
with the pretext of following courses at the Sorbonne. In spring 1911, at an
artists' colony at Koktebel in the Crimea, she encountered a tall, unbeliev-
ably handsome man, one year her junior, with a history of tuberculosis. He
came from a Jewish family with a tradition of revolutionary activism. It had
been scarred by tragedy when Sergey Efron's mother, returning home to
their Paris lodgings, found that one of her sons had hanged himself in the
bathroom, and immediately took her own life. Tsvetaeva married Efron in
January 1912. Their first daughter Ariadna (Alya) was born in September.
Two years later, the poet embarked on a turbulent relationship with Sofiya

Parnok, also a poet, which lasted a year and a half, provoking consternation among friends and acquaintances.

Having returned south with her husband, Tsvetaeva set off for Moscow once more, on November 25th. The outbreak of civil war effectively rendered her a prisoner in the capital. In January, Efron joined the counter-revolutionary forces as a volunteer. Tsvetaeva spent the years of War Communism camping out in the attic of a house she had moved to not long after getting married, in the room which had once been her husband's den. Long spells passed in which she had no news of him, yet she held on to the hope that he might be alive. They were finally reunited in Berlin, in June 1922.

Repeatedly, in both poems and notebooks, she describes 1919 as a plague year, one when the inhuman conditions of survival in the capital reached a nadir:

> My day: I get up – barest glimmer from the window in the roof – cold
> – puddles – sawdust – buckets - pitchers – dusters – little girl's skirts
> and blouses everywhere. I saw wood. Light the fire. Wash potatoes in
> icy water and cook them in the samovar, which I keep going with coals
> taken from the stove. (Day and night I wear the same dress of fustian,
> made for Asya in Alexandrov in spring 1917 while she was away, and
> which, one day, shrunk horrendously. It has burns all over, from fall-
> ing embers and cigarettes. Before, I kept the sleeves in place with an
> elastic band. Now they are rolled back and fastened with a safety pin.)

She had no running water, and neither lock nor key. Anyone who took the trouble to climb the stairs from the street could enter. A common thief, shocked at the misery he found, is said to have offered Tsvetaeva money.

Between 1918 and 1921, the population of St Petersburg may have fallen by as much as three quarters, and that of Moscow by half, so appalling were conditions in the cities. Of the peasant revolts which broke out, the most serious and extensive, in Tambov province, is thought to have led to nearly a quarter of a million deaths.

Against this background, surrounded by squalor, deprivation and despair, Tsvetaeva experienced moments of utter, piercing happiness:

> I forgot to write down what is most important: rejoicing, clarity of thoughts, delight at the smallest lucky break, plans for plays – the walls are scrawled all over with notes for a line of verse, with NBs for these notebooks!

She succeeded, so to speak, in contemplating life in the plague year through the wrong end of a telescope, in uncovering its emblematic, exemplary quality:

> Deprivation can seem infinitely cosy, a sort of dream. These days I live exactly as I choose: one room – an attic! – the sky close by, together with the children, Irina's toys, Alya's books – the samovar, the axe, the basket of potatoes – these are the main actors in life's play! My books, my jotters, a puddle from the leaking roof or a sunbeam spreading through the room – this is beyond time, it could be any time or any place – the eternal things are present: mother and children, poet and attic.

The years from 1917 to 1921 were arguably the most productive of her entire career. Her last collection had appeared in 1913. The next would not follow till 1921. The poet's American editors describe the uncollected poems from this period as a book in their own right, one whose contents could long only be guessed at. Tsvetaeva claimed different rivers fed into her work, as if into a sea. They may all be viewed here, in verses varying from the outstanding to the only moderately successful. Three extended cycles, addressed respectively to the actor and director Yury Zavadsky, the actress Sonya Holliday and the painter Nikolay Nikolayevich Vysheslavtsev, form a backbone.

Returning to Moscow from Crimea at the end of November, Tsvetaeva heard a poem recited in her carriage which made such an impression on her that she lost no time in contacting its author, Pavel Antokolsky. He introduced her to his friends at the Third Studio of the Moscow Art Theatre, which was under the leadership of Yevgeniy Vakhtangov. Tsvetaeva would compose no fewer than five verse dramas for them. Nearly two decades later, she would write that 'Pavel had a friend, about whom he talked constantly: Yury Z. "Me and Yura . . . When I read it to Yura . . . Yura always asks me . . . Yesterday Yura and I kissed each other provocatively, so people would believe Yura had at last fallen in love . . . Just imagine! Everyone in the studio rushes out and, instead of a young woman, who do they see? – Me!"' Though both would subsequently marry, and lead distinguished careers in Soviet theatre, Antokolsky and Zavadsky were at this stage lovers. Infatuation with a man who is not only unavailable, but gay, suffuses Tsvetaeva's 'Playacting' with an ironic, delightfully self-deprecating tone. This does not prevent her from reproaching herself bitterly, at its close, for self-indulgent philandering while her husband risked his life against the Bolsheviks.

A year later, in spring 1919, she gave a studio reading of her play *The Snow-*

storm. When she had finished, Pavel introduced her to a diminutive actress with an English surname, celebrated in Moscow for her performances of a monodrama based on Dostoevsky's *White Nights*. The 'Poems to Sonechka', however, are not, strictly speaking, addressed to Sonya. As Simon Karlinsky explains, what the poet does is stylise and parody the street ballads and sung romances, in execrable taste, which Sonya loved. The sixth poem is an exception. It reads like a foundation myth for the various forms of damaging and dysfunctional loving Tsvetaeva practised throughout her life. In 1937 the poet's daughter, having returned to the Soviet Union, passed on news of an emaciated Sonya's death from cancer. She had married a businessman who was devoted to her, but whom she did not love, spending the remainder of her life in the provinces. The upshot was a memoir, Tsvetaeva's most extended piece of prose, no less gushing and hopelessly romantic in approach than its subject had been, in which Volodya Alekseyev, the third member of a trinity formed with Zavadsky and Antokolsky, plays a major role. He disappeared not long after Easter 1919, presumably to join the counter-revolutionary forces, and was never heard of again.

Despite the acute nature of the predicaments she faced, as it became harder and harder to procure adequate supplies of food, Tsvetaeva could write of the plague year with rich humour: 'In the year 1919 people are surprised by nothing: the right time for me to be alive', 'I adore the year 1919, because I play at it.' She even planned an essay, to be called 'Justification of Evil', where she would list the benefits Bolshevism had brought. Her style of dress had always aroused disbelief, if not outrage, whereas she now could masquerade twenty-four hours a day without provoking consternation. One could die whenever one chose, merely by walking out into the street and crying *Vive le Roi!* Class boundaries were eliminated, not because a new ideology had come to dominate, but thanks to shared catastrophe – cold, hunger, disease – and a common hatred of the recently established rulers.

Many looked back to the French Revolution, as a comparable upheaval which could help one understand what was happening now. France of the *ancien régime* became a focus for generalised nostalgia about the lost world of Tsarist Russia. Not everyone survived, thanks to Tsvetaeva's inimitable blend of steely resilience and cavalier lack of responsibility. She saw in Alexey Alexandrovich Stakhovich, onetime courtier, actor and teacher of future actors, a relict of that world. When he hung himself in February 1919 she was deeply shocked. In 1916, the year of her meeting with Mandelstam, Tsvetaeva had written cycles of poems in homage to both Akhmatova and Aleksandr Blok. By contrast, her relationship with the symbolist poet and translator Konstantin Balmont was collegial in nature. Less isolated than she was, he lived with his wife and daughter, and could not understand why Tsvetaeva kept frustrating his repeated attempts to get her into bed. Her three poems to Vyacheslav Ivanov, high priest of symbolism, whose apartment in St Petersburg had hosted a famous literary salon, are distant in tone and reflect an increasing interest in disciplehood.

Despite her readiness to look on the plague year as a game ('What I like about adventurism is the word'), the year culminated in tragedy. Unwarily deceived by what she had been told about a state-run orphanage in Kuntsevo, on Moscow's outskirts, Tsvetaeva left both her daughters there in December, under the fond illusion they would be better looked after than at home. Even in the notes she kept while away, Alya took care never to refer to Tsvetaeva as her mother. In the new year, news came that Alya had contracted malaria. Tsvetaeva brought her elder daughter home, and nursed her through fever after fever. In the interim Irina died of malnutrition. Tsvetaeva did not return to the orphanage, and made no attempt to find out where her daughter had been buried. Her sisters-in-law laid the blame for Irina's wretched existence, and still more wretched death, firmly at her mother's door. The poet's notebooks suggest she faced no more severe judge than her own conscience. Years later, she could still observe that, if a child of yours has starved to death, you never feel people have eaten enough.

A note of desperation, of forcing, detectable in the poems to Vysheslavtsev, which date from April and May 1920, should come as no surprise. Going on indications in the notebooks, the epigraphs are snippets from the painter's conversation, on which individual poems expand and comment. None of her three infatuations found sexual realisation. With Zavadsky, things did not proceed beyond endless and obsessive kissing. Tsvetaeva merely sat at the severe, forbidding, Vysheslavtsev's knees, letting him run his hands through her hair. Her sexual encounters in these years, if her four-line poems are to be believed, were predominantly casual and short-lived in nature. Images in the third cycle, of a ship's boy clambering up the rigging, a tightrope walker and a dancer, suggest a disquieting degree of masochistic theatricality, of aggressively putting on a show. It makes for uneasy reading, as does the overwhelming self-disgust setting in near the close.

These are only some of the strands running through Tsvetaeva's poems of the plague year. Her *alter egos* include a drummer boy idolising Napoleon; an irrepressibly mischievous grandmother, who refuses to apologise to God on judgement day (Tsvetaeva observed that, seen through a woman's eyes, God is the equivalent of an ageing husband); and a Joan of Arc whose androgyny renders her more fascinating. There are instances of folk speech, and dialect inflections, along with incursions into an exotic Orient, or stylised evocations of ancient Russia. Tsvetaeva is consistently preoccupied by victimhood, predominantly but not exclusively female, in all its various manifestations. It would be a grave error, however, to forget that she is an enormously funny poet, with an unrivalled and infectious sense of humour. This, as much as any other quality, can explain her success in not only reaching the end of the plague year alive, but making it among the most fruitful in her entire career. As one of her four-liners has it:

> While your eyes follow me into the grave,
> write up the whole caboodle on my cross!
> 'Her days began with songs, ended in tears,
> but when she died, she split her sides with laughter!'

Note on This Book

The boundaries of the plague year have been stretched, in order to encompass Tsvetaeva's three major cycles. All the shorter poems she completed between November 1918 and May 1920 are included. A majority of these poems appear in English for the first time, offering readers an in-depth cross-section of Tsvetaeva's work. Six appeared in *Milestones 2* (Moscow 1921), six in *Psyche* (Berlin 1923) and six in *The Swan's Encampment* (not published until 1957). A further two appear in both the latter books. More than one hundred items remained in manuscript at the poet's death, several not achieving publication till as late as 1990 or 1994. A generous selection of incomplete or fragmentary poems is also included, with missing words or lines indicated [...], and editorial suggestions thus [dancer's]. These items might tempt one to posit a perfectionist Tsvetaeva, allowing days and days to pass as she struggles to find precisely the right phrase or word. She speaks of doing this in a later letter, but a passage from the notebooks for these years offers a totally different explanation:

> I never need to look for poems. Poems come to me, and what's more, in such abundance that I haven't the faintest notion what to write, what to discard.
>
> Which accounts for all my unfinished, and unwritten poems.
>
> Sometimes what I do is begin a poem on the right side of the page, another on the left, then somewhere alongside a line from a third poem, my hand flies across from one place to the other, flies all over

the page, breaking off one poem to push ahead with another – chasing after, catching hold, so as not to forget! There isn't enough time – *my hand can't keep up!*

The translator is grateful to Tania Retivov and Katalin Szőke, who offered their interpretation of particularly puzzling passages. Tanya Filosofova carefully checked the entire final draft against the original Russian text.

Budapest, December 2012

archipelago books

is a not-for-profit literary press devoted to
promoting cross-cultural exchange through innovative
classic and contemporary international literature
www.archipelagobooks.org